A Definition of Tragedy

A DEFINITION OF

Tragedy

By OSCAR MANDEL

NEW YORK UNIVERSITY PRESS   1961

AN EARLIER FORM *of Chapter 6 of this book was published in the University of Kansas City Review (Spring 1959). Permission to reprint some of this material is gratefully acknowledged.*

Reprinted 1968

AUTHOR'S NOTE

IN THE PROCESS of defining the term tragedy, I have used and quoted from an international, though always Western, miscellany of works. But the reader should perhaps be cautioned that he will not find in this essay an analysis of any literary work as such. The focus remains on the theory of tragedy, for which each reader can supply his own examples. At the same time, however, I am conscious of the fact that in the choice of my illustrations I have been negligent of a number of authors to whom the modern reader has a certain right to expect some allusion; and were I to begin again, I should certainly draw more heavily on recent authors: on Brecht especially, on Pirandello, Mann, Mauriac, O'Neill, Montherlant, Hemingway, Faulkner, and many another wit of this century who has "touched the lyre in honour of the Tragic Muse."

REFERENCES in the footnotes are given by name and page number only, with the exception of a few works outside the field of tragedy for which bibliographic information is supplied *in situ*. For a full bibliographic description of the works used in this essay the reader can turn to the list of books at the end of the volume. The translations throughout are the author's except where credit is given, either in the footnotes or in the bibliography.

Los Angeles, 1961

CONTENTS

Part One

Part Two

A Definition of Tragedy

Part One

1 · Basic Method

DISCUSSIONS of tragedy are numberless; definitions of the term few; and of those, only one has endured longer than the attacks against it. No one thinks that Aristotle's definition is perfect, and many students do not like it at all; yet it is impossible to write at any length on tragedy without referring back to that first and most fruitful approach. It is possible, on the other hand—and even easy—to ignore any of the later writers on this subject, with the exception of Hegel. What recommends Aristotle is his utter sanity. He never allows us, as rhapsodical writers do, to gain the impression that he is overwhelmed by any of his subjects. His air of command is such that one could almost believe he had created the world he is so easy in. Still, this has not helped to perpetuate his philosophical or scientific opinions, simply because in the sciences and even in philosophy there is an evolution: the new does not sit beside the old, it often superannuates it. But the arts are essentially unprogressive, and a dictum about art published two thousand years ago has as good a chance of being valid as one delivered today. That is one reason why this almost incidental piece of Aristotle's is, of all his writings, the one which claims today a completely uncondescending, unhistoric consideration. It is useful, no doubt, to describe the limitations of Aristotle's analysis which are due to historic conditions; but when that is done, and a few details are cleared away, we remain with a document which has not yet been superseded; certainly one which cannot be ignored.

Recent comprehensive definitions are very scarce. Particularly

in this century, students of literature have preferred to deal with
aspects of tragedy or with periods of tragedy rather than with
the problem of what, precisely, is meant when the term tragedy
is used. There is of course a large literature on, say, the charac-
teristics or the sources of Elizabethan or French tragedy; there
are many considerations of the philosophical repercussions of
tragedy, of the psychological effect of tragedy, and on the possibility of modern tragedy. Most of the time the assumption
seems to be that we all know, after all, what a tragic work is
when we meet with one. For the rest, the definitions which do
occur in contemporary works often look like *obiter dicta,* so that
it seems a little unfair to lift them out of their contexts and to
exhibit them as though they were serious attempts at analysis.
But since nothing else is available, we may as well glance at a
few twentieth-century insights.

We are told, for example, that "a typical tragedy is concerned
with a great personality engaged in a struggle that ends dis-
astrously"; [1] that "tragedy . . . is a representation of human unhappiness which pleases us notwithstanding, by the truth with
which it is seen and the skill with which it is communicated"; [2]
or that "the essential tragic idea [consists in] climax followed by
decline, or pride by judgment." [3] Elsewhere tragedy is spoken of
as "the arousing in the reader of a noble mixture of pity and
fear, usually accomplished through a worldly conflict; and a significant, meaningful, because true, interpretation of life." [4] We
hear of tragedy as a preoccupation "with the more serious, enig-
matic or afflicting circumstances of life," [5] or as "a fiction inspired by a serious concern with the problem of man's fate." [6]
Again, tragedy is said to be "always a clash of two powers—
necessity without, freedom within; outside, a great, rigid, arbitrary law of fate; inside, the undefeated individual will, which
can win its spiritual triumph even when all its material sur-

1 Thorndike, p. 9.
2 Lucas, p. 58.
3 G. Murray, p. 60.
4 Ekeberg, p. 7.
5 Dixon, p. 11.
6 Muller, p. 14.

roundings and environment have crumbled into hopeless ruin"; [7] or else, to conclude, "a spectacle of a constant and inevitable relation between good and evil, a dramatic representation of a law of values" [8]—to wit, that in the upshot the amount of good and pleasure balances precisely the amount of evil and grief.

These are a few of the modern definitions in the English language—in which, by the way, most of the recent criticism seems to be written. They strike one as either casual, pseudo-profound, or so broad as to encompass almost all serious, and a good deal of comic, literature. Writers on this subject often assume a solemn vagueness which impresses the reader and possibly inspires him with awe; but in the end their approach is discouragingly useless compared with the simple, precise and cold statements of Aristotle. I should add that, refreshingly, the best modern work on tragedy, Johannes Volkelt's *Asthetik des Tragischen*, provides no definition at all. A few others feel that tragedy has gone beyond definition, and that one had better proceed at once to a discussion of subjects under the undefinable category. [9] The present study naturally assumes that definition is still possible, in spite of the mass of experiences which have come forward under the name of tragedy since the Greek spoke. It assumes too, and safely enough, that Aristotle's definition, satisfying though it is, does not house all the objects which deserve a place in the tragic mansion. If the Church can allow notions such as sin or grace to grow, to change, to involve new and abandon old objects, we can imagine an ancient category of art such as tragedy also evolving, and yet not so strangely as to lose its name.

THE TERM "TRAGEDY" has two very distinct uses. In everyday and newspaper practice, it is a synonym for calamity. Among readers of books, it signifies the large notions we have just mentioned,

7 Courtney, p. 12.
8 Myers, p. 8.
9 E.g., Henn, p. 282: "There neither is nor can be any definition of tragedy that is sufficiently wide to cover its variant forms in the history of world literature."

certain cosmic implications, sadness coupled with grandeur, powerful effects, or a few structural rules, usually pseudo-Aristotelian. Now the first, the popular meaning of tragedy, cannot be touched. My purpose, rather, is to make definite and therefore useful its diffuse literary meanings; to attach to the word what is called a "stipulative definition"—removing ambiguities and refreshing, so to speak, an old and much-travelled concept: "a sort of turning our backs to reality in order to approach it again with a new set of conceptions that will give us a better grasp of the facts." [10] Naturally, it would be absurd to propose a definition thrusting out of the canon a host of works which everyone has always taken for tragedies. The word we are dealing with has after all been attached to a certain number of known objects—in particular the serious drama of Periclean Athens, of Shakespeare, and of Racine—so long and indeed so honorably that our definition must encompass them or else banish itself to the limbo of critical eccentricities. Our question cannot be, "Is *Othello* a tragedy?" It must be, "What is it about *Othello* which makes it tragic?" Obvious as this may seem, it should be remembered that in the course of critical history, men of reputation have taken it upon themselves to relegate to the nontragic territory works which, as it turned out, could not be moved. Those who could not accept Shakespeare or Racine as true tragic authors merely removed themselves from intellectual intercourse with mankind. And yet, the function of definition, if it has any, is precisely to make such intercourse possible.

In short, when the definer is dealing with a word pointing inexorably to a certain number of objects, he cannot freely choose his referends; he can only bring to light the similar components among the referends which have attracted the single term used for them; and this exploration, this *ex post facto* analysis, this return of the mind onto its own behavior, is properly the work of definition.

Needless to say, the definer, whatever his doctrine, will not be able to admit the entrance of *all* works which have been called tragedies at one time or another. The very haziness of the word, the casual way in which, because it is an honorific term, it has

10 Richard Robinson, *Definition*, Oxford: Clarendon Press, 1950, p. 69.

been employed, the multifarious definitions it has endured, fore-ordain that, after accepting the works of art which it would be critical suicide to bar, the definer will be compelled in turn to select and to reject. In fact, were it not so—were there never any doubt about the tragic nature of a given work—there would be no question of definition to begin with. To make the word serviceable, we must prune, though we must be on guard against lopping.

With this in mind, the definer undertakes to read as many supposed tragedies as he can; to which he adds a sufficient number of doubtful, impossible, and "halfway" works. At an early stage of his study, he is likely to form an hypothesis, which he may eventually replace by another, or which he may amend and improve as he continues to read. Ultimately, if he is successful, he will find that he has in hand a statement which seems to fulfill the requirements for a definition. For it represents the common denominator of a substantial majority of works that in the past, for one reason or another, have been referred to as tragedies; and this, as we have seen, is the *sine qua non* of the definition which he desires. Furthermore, the statement represents a *minimum* common denominator. Not a few of the definitions current today are broad enough to cover melodrama, intrigue, and sometimes even comedy.[11] If tragedy is defined so generously that all serious art turns out to be tragic, we lose the fact that among serious works differences so remarkable exist that they exact from us separate terms; and is it not the function of language to capture for the use of mankind the *differentiae* which matter, or may matter, to man?

It follows, then, that the term tragedy, if it does probe into the realm of serious art to carve out a specific area within it, should refer to something that matters. The object—the refer-end—must have importance. Tragedy, in short, ought to be a symbol exchangeable for a set of symbols (say a sentence) pointing by general consent to a referend which is—again by general consent—worth pointing to. Thus, the set of symbols

11 E.g., the definition of tragedy as "a representation of an interdepend-ence of events (*Geschehenszusammenhang*) through the interaction of man and happiness and misery," in Mann, p. 13.

will not consist of a mere collection of external rules, nor in some trifling idea which can be of interest to no one but the pedant. It must point to a reality of earthly existence which no thinker can neglect. And the discovery that this important human idea provides the identity among works of art in all forms, of all nationalities, of cultures almost unaware of each other, gives the definition the justification for its existence.

It is then, finally, only the importance of the concept of tragedy which makes the task of stating it more than a pedantic exercise. If the least common denominator among a host of works denominated as tragedies in the past turns out to be a verbal trifle, then we may indeed be indifferent to the question whether *Death of a Salesman* or *A Streetcar Named Desire* belongs to the genre or not. When, however, to be tragic means to partake of an idea or an emotion which is commonly held to have genuine consequence in reality, classification becomes interesting. And all men feel, of course, even before attempting a definition, that the term must refer to some matter of consequence, and that we are right in wishing to preserve it and to continue using it. That is why, as has been pointed out elsewhere, [12] artists often misapply this honorific name (as they misapply the word symphony or sonnet) to a new work of theirs, taking advantage of its vagueness to exploit its benefits.

In sum, the definition must keep in equipoise three requirements. First, it must be expansive enough to include as many of the hitherto proposed referends as possible; second, however, it must be economical and seek out only the elements which differentiate these referends from a larger significant group (such as "serious drama"); and third, the *differentiae* so discovered, which constitute the definition, must justify their claim to an independent term—tragedy—by their possession of human significance. Thus, a definition of tragedy as the exhibition of man in the toils of fortune and misfortune conforms to the first and third, but violates the second requirement; the definition which includes a demand for unity of time violates the first; a definition which claimed that tragedy is a verbal exercise would violate the third. Our chief concern in this essay is with the violation of the second requirement, economy, in favor of the first,

12 Jarrett, pp. 195–96.

inclusiveness—a violation which has led to a confusion between the serious and the tragic; and our attempt will be to isolate from the larger group the tragic subgroup and to show the significant *differentiae* which mark it out.

The inquiry which follows limits itself neither with regard to epoch nor with regard to nationality. It rests rather on the unity of the human race and even the essential unity of its expressions. "Taste in Paris turned out to be like that of Athens," Racine wrote on one occasion. That was an exaggeration, no doubt; yet we may assume that man has grown no new emotions since Homer's day, and we will look for the tragic event from the *Iliad* to *La Peste* without even a sense of boldness. Tastes indeed have changed, and subject matters have come and gone; whole philosophies, whole religions, once the staples of art, have made way for others; the titans have yielded to the clerks, ambition has yielded to loneliness, Christianity to existentialism, the troubadour to the novelist; yet for all that, our inquiry will seek out identity and not development.

Neither will we discuss the history of tragic literature; we will only touch on the history of the aesthetics of tragedy; and we will attempt no analysis of individual works or epochs. Finally— and most important—illustrations will be drawn from every form: the drama, the novel, the poem, the short story. For example, we curtly abolish the distinction between the epic and tragedy, which has about as much validity as a distinction between the sonnet and onomatopoeia (*Paradise Lost* is a tragic epic, the *Lusiads* is a serious epic, and the *Odyssey* is a serio-comic epic). No reason has yet been discovered for making an idea about human existence a preserve for one kind of art. We could, in fact, speak of tragic painting and sculpture without changing a word of our definition. Our field, however, is literature; this far, and no further, we limit the scope of this essay.[13]

13 Several recent works, and most notably Otto Mann's *Poetik der Tragödie*, still assume that tragedy is one of the *dramatic* forms; that tragedy is limited to the *staging* of a human idea. The absurdity of this restriction is shown by Lessing's reason for it: "Aristotle perceived that pity necessarily required a present evil, that evils which happened long ago or threaten in the distant future are not at all commiserated by us, or at any rate not as much as present ones, and that it was consequently necessary to represent the action which is to arouse our pity not as past but as present— that is to say, not in the narrative but in the dramatic form." (No. 77.)

2 · Types of Definition

AN EXAMINATION of historic definitions discloses two basically divergent approaches to the problem, leading to two general types of definition. The first we shall call *derivative* definitions, and the second *substantive* definitions.

A derivative definition is one which postulates an *a priori* order, usually ontological, of which tragedy is an expression. The definition is then characteristically nonaesthetic, though of course it may include aesthetic requirements. Instead of asking what tragedy expresses, the derivative definition tends to ask what expresses itself through tragedy. The cosmic order is not discovered by means of the work of art; on the contrary, it exists previous to the work and merely asks the work to dramatize it. The critic (or theologian) may flatly demand that tragedy make it its business to convey a pre-established doctrine. Subtler critics may assert that tragedy does in fact consciously or unconsciously mirror the doctrine, for it is, in a manner of speaking, an exudation of Being. Tragedy is umbilically attached to a mothering intellectual system, and incomprehensible without it.

Substantive definitions, on the other hand, begin with the work of art itself. If substantive critics discover an ontological order in it—and they all too often do—the point is that the order is precisely *in* the work. Such critics are interested in the constituent elements of art, rather than its ontological sources. But they differ widely in their emphases; they may look at the work of art from opposite poles, and with different techniques. We may, in fact, range under substantive definitions four ap-

proaches, though each represents a particular emphasis rather
than antagonism to the others.

A] *Definition by formal elements.* The emphasis here is on
rules — for example, legislation on the three unities, diction, or
the hero's social level.

B] *Definition by situation.* What *happens* in tragedy? What
is its recurrent subject matter, its internal concept? A simple
instance of this class is the definition of tragedy as a kind of
work exhibiting the fall of a good man.

C] *Definition by ethical direction.* Not so much what happens literally, but what is the thematic implication of the work,
concerns the critic here. The question is, what does tragedy
mean? Our interest is in the intellectual and moral effect of our
genre. A common example is the definition which asserts that
tragedy expresses the nobility of man. It is not always easy to
keep this class of definition distinct from derivative definitions.
The test is whether the ontological or ethical order emerges
from the text, or whether the text merely echoes or dramatizes a
pre-established order.

D] *Definition by emotional effect.* The illustrious example
here is, of course, Aristotle's requirement of pity and fear, and
the elimination of both from our nervous system.

These four subclasses, it goes without saying, are not mutually exclusive, but they show the directions in which investi-
gators have pushed deepest, each his own way. The third approach, in particular, has been pursued with such insistence in
our generation that the track has become a boulevard on which
easy profundities travel without encumbrance.

The history of tragic conceptions exhibits itself, remarkably
enough, as a cycle in which the derivative and substantive—or
deductive and empirical—definitions alternate. The Aristotelian
definition, with the school it founded, its scholiasts, and Horace,
is a substantive one. This is followed by the medieval school of
tragedy, in which the narrative exemplifies an orthodoxy concerning the sublunar world, namely that the latter is "ruled by
Fortune, the irrational spirit of chance," [1] a concept which in its
turn depends upon a whole theology.

1 Farnham, p. 78.

Thus starf this worthy mighty Hercules;
Lo, who may truste on fortune any throwe?
For him that folweth al this world of prees,
Er he be war, is ofte y-leyd ful lowe.

So writes Chaucer, whose Troilus also learned the lesson after
his death, hearing heavenly harmonies in the seventh sphere,

. . . and fully gan despyse
This wrecched world, and held al vanitee
To respect of the pleyn felicitee
That is in hevene above.

The next body of critical ukases is the neo-, or rather the
pseudo-, Aristotelian one of the Renaissance and the French
classicists. Reading and interpreting Aristotle, who had presumably found Nature out, these critics developed in effect a new
definition of tragedy, which was substantive once more: the
still-familiar code of princely heroes, eloquent passions, the unities, decorum; a world, in short, of formal rules:

. . . nous, que la raison à ses règles engage,
Nous voulons qu'avec art l'action se ménage. . . .[2]
—rules sometimes as minute and tough as those in Deuteron-
omy, sometimes, like Racine's, rather "poetical": "Il suffit que
l'action en soit grande, que les acteurs en soient héroiques, que
les passions y soient excitées, et que tout s'y ressente de cette
tristesse majestueuse qui fait tout le plaisir de la tragédie." [3]
Here again tragedy had become a self-sustaining earthly entity,
subject to the scrutiny not of theologians but of spectators.

Classical definitions held their own until the German idealists
provided a new approach, and this time the cycle swung back to
the definition by derivation. Schelling we may regard as one of
the pacemakers. "The philosophy of art is the science of the
Whole in the form or power [aspect] of art." [4] Therefore, logi-

2 "Bound to reason's rules, we wish the action to be developed with
art." Boileau, III, 43–44.
3 "It is enough that the action be great, the actors heroic, the passions
excited, and that everything exhibit the majestic sadness in which the
pleasure of tragedy consists." Racine, p. 483.
4 Schelling, p. 16.

cally enough, he begins his study of art with a close exposition
of his metaphysic. For Schelling, only metaphysics—not psychology, and not mere aesthetics—can supply the *Urquellen*, the
primal sources, of art. As philosophy discloses the Absolute or
God under the aspect (*Potenz*) of truth, so art discloses it under
the aspect of beauty, though it is understood—as Keats was to
understand rather vaguely—that truth and beauty (and goodness, for that matter) are all one, since the Absolute is indi-
visibly one. A human work like tragedy can be understood only,
and defined only, in its relation to the Absolute. "For art is
shown to be the true representation of the form of things as they
are in themselves—that is to say, of the forms of the Primal
Images" (*Urbilder*).[5] The latter, needless to say, are God or the
Absolute under the aspect of eternal beauty. Man imitates in
art the supernal beauty of God. When Schelling concludes one
of his lectures with the statement that art is an emanation
(*Ausfluss*) of the Absolute, he speaks for several generations of
Teutonic theorists. To enumerate their definitions or descrip-
tions, and set one to quarrel or agree with the other, is too
otiose a task for our century. A few samples must be enough for
us. Take Schelling again: "What matters in Tragedy is a real
conflict of freedom in the subject and necessity as objective,
which conflict does not end with the defeat of one or the other,
but with the simultaneous appearance in complete indifference,
and victory and defeat of both." [6] This, like the medieval Wheel
of Fortune, rests on a metaphysic in which indifference is a
technical term for the Absolute, and the subject and object—
freedom and necessity—are its two arms, which the protagonists
and antagonists make concrete. Schlegel speaks of "a higher
order of things, impressed on the apparently irregular course of
events, and mysteriously revealed in them." [7] And again, "The
subject of tragedy (properly speaking) is the struggle between
the outward finite existence, and the inward infinite aspirations." [8] For Hegel, tragedy portrays "the divine in its secular or

5 *Ibid.*, p. 35.
6 *Ibid.*, p. 341.
7 Schlegel, p. 69.
8 *Ibid.*, p. 177.

worldly realization." [9] The blessed spirit of the universe is un-
molested by conflicts, but it already contains an impulse to
"transplant itself in the real actuality of the phenomenal
world." [10] It becomes differentiated, though presumably all its
strands still partake of the spirit's beneficent nature. Unfortunately, the same strands, or ethical principles, tend to become
self-assertive: one clashes with the other in this reaching out for
supremacy. Eventually, justice reimposes the ethical substance
through the downfall "of the individuality which disturbs its repose." [11] So much for what Lucas calls the "Universe squirted
with philosophic rose-water," in which the fall of individuals
demands no tear, for through their fall the ethical substance is
once more pacified.

As a more poetic German, we may cite Nietzsche, who also
begins with a Primordial Being which is, to put it mildly, explo-
sive. Dionysian tragedy represents this Being's "raging desire for
existence and joy in existence; the struggle, the pain, the destruction of phenomena, now appear to us as a necessary thing, in
view of the countless forms of existence which force and push
one another into life, in view of the exuberant fertility of the
universal will." [12] For the human being, the villain here is again
individuation, the breaking up of unity. We are likely to regard
the great, dark force with gloom; but art, and in particular
tragedy, comes as the redeemer into this "Dionysian abyss." It
shows us the primacy of the eternal undifferentiated life, demonstrates the unimportance of a single man's death—nay, very
often the need for it, as seen from the viewpoint of the infinite
turbulence, and teaches us to view "the playful construction and
demolishing of the world of individuals as the overflow of a
primitive delight." [13]

Finally, we may briefly cite Schopenhauer, to whom tragedy
is the "representation of the terrible side of life. The unspeak-
able pain, the wail of humanity, the triumph of evil, the scorn-
ful mastery of chance, and the irretrievable fall of the just and

9 Hegel, p. 296.
10 Ibid., p. 297.
11 Ibid., p. 298.
12 Nietzsche, p. 279.
13 Ibid., p. 337.

innocent, is here presented to us; and in this lies a significant hint of the nature of the world and existence." [14] Tragedy, as far as Schopenhauer is concerned, represents the blind will—which is the Absolute—in action; and by showing the horror of that action, how good it were to deny It. The nature of tragedy therefore is not intelligible except as an enactment of the evil or blind cosmic will; an affirmative work could not be tragic; and the reading of *Oedipus* without reference to the absolute source of reality is not only inadequate but downright evil.[15]

As German idealism waned, the wheel took one more turn. In the twentieth century the trend has been once more toward a definition by analysis of the internal theme and elements; discussions of the stature of the hero, the emotional effect, diction, aesthetic pleasure, and the like.[16] This is to be expected, of course, in an age which has divorced art from all other disciplines, and especially from theology and ethics; an age which glorifies art's autonomy or—in plain English—uselessness (the most useful part of a house, said Gautier in a notable pronouncement, is the water closet). For all that, as we have seen, our century has failed to produce a definition of tragedy which, using Aristotle's calm method, could gain secular favor and finally replace his formulation.

The single exception to substantive definitions in our age is provided, perhaps, by the so-called archetypal critics. It is hard to say whether these scholars are really concerned with definition, but they discuss tragedy as expressions, often unconscious, of a pre-established order. Characteristically, however, the order is neither ontological nor ethical, but psychological. Tragedy revives a myth which is itself the expression of an ineradicable human concept or emotion. The tragic hero is the Vegetation God who is born, who waxes, who decays (or sins), and who is slain by his successor—another like himself—and then reborn. Tragedy rose out of the song-and-dance ritual (*molpé*) celebrat-

14 Schopenhauer, I, 326.

15 Fanciers of German theory can read the works of Solger, Zeising, Vischer, Hartmann, and a number of others. The *principle* of the German theorists is sufficiently illustrated by those we have mentioned.

16 In Germany, the reversal is marked in the works of Dehmel, Volkelt and Mann. See notably Mann, PI. IV, chs. 3–4.

ing this cycle, and when we witness the tragedy of Orestes or of Hamlet, something, we know not what, in the depth of us is stirred, as by a mysteriously significant ritual, for we all float in the stream of the "racial consciousness." "The mystery of our response to tragedy . . . is thus given a deeply rooted psychological basis which in its turn is found buried in the innermost layers of the group consciousness." [17] In tragedy, we die with the hero and then we are resurrected with him. For a while, like the celebrants of the ancient mysteries, we become the god himself.

If this archetype does not suit us, however, we are offered another, to wit the conflict between two simultaneous emotional tendencies or selves: "the self of imaginative aspiration" or "power craving" against "the surrender of personal claims and the merging of the ego within a greater power—the 'community consciousness.' " We are given to understand that "the archetypal pattern corresponding to tragedy may be said to be a certain organization of the tendencies of self-assertion and submission." [18] These tendencies are ancestral; they appear as "the sense of guilt which haunts the child whose emerging self-will drives him into collision with his parents." [19] The contradictory feelings are given relief in the tragic ritual. "Our exultation in the death of Hamlet is related in direct line of descent to the religious exultation felt by the primitive group that made sacrifice of the divine king or sacred animal, the representative of the tribal life, and, by the communion of its shed blood, felt that life strengthened and renewed." [20] Hamlet and Orestes and Oedipus are either Vegetation Gods who kill their "fathers" or predecessors—the old sinful Year—while the Mother looks on; or else they represent power versus submission, and the final "merging of the ego within a greater power." Or indeed they are both.

However this may be, and whether or not we are dealing here with serious attempts at definition of a genre, the dependence

17 Weisinger, p. 26.
18 Bodkin, p. 23.
19 *Ibid.*, p. 60.
20 *Ibid.*, p. 21.

of this view of tragedy on a pre-established, if entirely natural, order is obvious. Like all such conceptions, it depends for its existence on the reality of the postulated order—in this case, on the reality of these subterranean emotions of ours. And just as tragedy to the medievals became a kind of documentation of orthodox theology, so to these students tragedy appears as an enactment of permanent racial verities.

As a possible footnote to the archetypal system, the work of Suzanne Langer might be mentioned, though it is hard to classify. If her approach to tragedy is derivative (in our sense of the term), the pre-established order is neither metaphysical, ethical, nor anthropological-psychological, but properly biological: "Drama abstracts from reality the fundamental forms of consciousness: the first reflection of natural activity in sensation, awareness, and expectation, which belongs to all higher creatures and might be called, therefore, the pure sense of life; and beyond that, the reflection of an activity, which is at once more elaborate, and more integrated, having a beginning, efflorescence, and end—the personal sense of life, or self-realization." Thus, drama is founded on, or derived from, the universal-fundamental *doing* of the higher creature. This leads Miss Langer into a discussion of comedy far more satisfying than her analysis of tragedy. Tragedy turns out to be nothing but the transference of the rhythm already mentioned; this rhythm is "exemplified in mental and emotional growth, maturation, and the final relinquishment of power" in a foreshortened dramatic action. Tragedy abstracts this rhythm and "imprints" it on what we call subject matter. "The big unfolding of feeling in the organic, personal pattern of a human life, rising, growing, accomplishing destiny and meeting doom—that is tragedy." [21]

I place this approach to tragedy among derivative definitions with some qualms, for it might be arrived at by a mere study of texts, and thus become a substantive definition by situation. But Miss Langer seems to *arrive at* tragedy, and to look upon it, almost as the medievals did, as though it were an *exemplum* emitted by the larger, basic order of things. In any event, the shortcoming of this definition is simply that it is too

21 Langer, pp. 327, 356, 366.

broad. It can be conjured away with the mere remark that it allows the hero to be a downright Satan, since in the latter the same pattern of growth and decay, and the same ordering of events by what Miss Langer calls Fate (meaning a control which eliminates accidents) can be manifest.

THE VIEW proposed in this essay belongs to the Aristotelian or nonmetaphysical tradition. It professes ignorance of the true nature of reality, hence cannot suppose tragedy, or indeed art itself, to be the manifestation or the working out of a specific ontological system. Milton, in his *Areopagitica*, tells the story of the wicked deceivers, who "took the virgin Truth, hewed her lovely form into a thousand pieces, and scattered them to the four winds"; and how "from that time ever since, the sad friends of Truth, such as durst appear, imitating the careful search that Isis made for the mangled body of Osiris, went up and down gathering up limb by limb still as they could find them." Those who believe that the body is fragmented, and furthermore that we shall never see it whole, do not derive art from a cosmic system, or criticize a particular work as it conforms to the system or departs from it. They resort rather to a decent ethic which may not be "proved" but which is seldom challenged, and to the scattered truths we observe rather than the Truth we construct. This modest approach "allows" the artist to teach or to use any metaphysical order he chooses, for it does not establish its categories, or issue its norms, under any nonaesthetic order whatsoever.

By the same token, we shall avoid definitions which depend for their very existence on certain psychological, historical, or biological facts, no matter how securely anchored these facts may appear to be. To discuss Hegel's definition of tragedy, we must first make sure that there really is an ethical Substance which seeks to resume its integrity against the overweening claims of its individual members. To discuss the Jungian views, we must ascertain whether we really participate unconsciously in the agricological interests of our forefathers and whether our unconscious really recognizes and thrills to the rehearsal of basic life patterns. Definitions by derivation fall if the order behind them falls; while, unfortunately, they by no means necessarily stand if the order stands. For if Hegel's definition leaves out of account much of the drama we have always called tragic, so do definitions which rely on the killing of the Vegetation God or the immersion of the spectator, like a character in Durkheim, in the tribal consciousness. We may criticize these views, then, by their intrinsic weaknesses as well as *a priori* by their dependence on matters not in the texts of the plays themselves. We will rather rely for our definition on the texts, and only the texts. For if Aristotle, as Gilbert Murray admits, had forgotten the primitive origins and the mythical significance of Greek tragedy, we may safely follow him, and listen to Hamlet without expecting in our souls echoes of primeval rages or aboriginal satisfactions. The origin of an object is not the same thing as its substance. In Hamlet, the Vegetation God is not only transcended, but, like a snake's skin, molted, abandoned, and forgotten.

3 · The Definition

SO FAR, then, we walk in the footsteps of Aristotle: our definition is to be purely aesthetic; it is to depend for its existence on no other discipline, and on no fact undiscoverable in the texts themselves; it is to emerge, like Aristotle's, simply from experience with the texts, as though we had never thought about "higher questions." Again, this definition will set tragedy at liberty to exhibit any ontological or ethical order which is not directly incompatible with the terms of tragedy; and the field, as we shall see, is large.

The following, then, is a substantive definition by situation.[1] It purports to be perfectly economical, admitting not a single word which is not absolutely required by the case.

A work of art is tragic if it substantiates the following situation: *A protagonist who commands our earnest good will is impelled in a given world by a purpose, or undertakes an action, of a certain seriousness and magnitude; and by that very purpose or action, subject to that same given world, necessarily and inevitably meets with grave spiritual or physical suffering.*

This definition is not meant to startle; in one or two respects it repeats the unpretentious Aristotelian concept. But what is worth stressing once more is that the statement represents the *whole* definition; that, whatever else the tragic work may say, only this is properly tragic, only this exhausts the identity among all tragedies. By the same token, whatever the statement

[1] See p. 11.

omits—and it is quiet on many subjects—is therefore not properly an ingredient in the essence of tragedy. Tragedy, as we have seen already, has been an ideal site for lofty intellectual constructions, but the builders have more than once been tempted to build high rather than well. The modesty of the definition proposed here must justify itself in the sequel: we are to explore the possibility of maintaining a view of tragedy which does not slip into rhapsody.

It may be useful at this point to present Aristotle's concept as well as the modified concept suggested by S. H. Butcher, though the latter intends to be faithful to his master.

What follows is a *composite* definition drawn from Butcher's and Bywater's translations of the *Poetics*. It makes use of various portions of Aristotle's analysis instead of limiting itself to the well-known central paragraph (1449 b), and it attempts to distinguish with great care between what Aristotle seems to regard as essential—that is to say, as part of the definition—and elements which he regards as merely useful or commendable.

"Tragedy, then, is an imitation of a single, unified action that is serious, complete, probable [we might say "plausible" nowadays] and of a certain magnitude; concerning the fall of a man whose character is good (though not pre-eminently just or virtuous), appropriate, believable and consistent; whose misfortune is brought about not by vice or depravity but by some error or frailty; in language embellished with each kind of artistic ornament, the several kinds being found in separate parts of the play; in the form of an action, not of narrative; with incidents arousing pity and fear, wherewith to accomplish the catharsis of these emotions." [2]

Let us set beside this Butcher's own view, though it too, like so many modern definitions, is given rather casually, in this case in the midst of a discussion of the martyr as a tragic hero.

"Tragedy, in its pure idea, shows us a mortal will engaged in an unequal struggle with destiny, whether that destiny be represented by the forces within or without the mind. The conflict

[2] This definition draws on sections 1449 b, 1451 a, 1451 b, 1453 a, and 1454 a of the *Poetics*.

reaches its tragic issue when the individual perishes, but through his ruin the disturbed order of the world is restored and the moral forces reassert their sway." [3]

The chief point to be observed in connection with the three definitions is that Aristotle includes an emotional effect, Butcher an ethical direction, and the proposed definition neither. We will return to these points in later sections, and turn our attention for the moment to the center of the proposed definition.

3 Butcher, pp. 311–12.

4 · The Kernel of the Definition

THE IDEA of tragedy proposed here is not a literary artifact,
like the three unities, but a reality. It is very seldom, of course,
that we encounter in life the completeness and the purity of
literature. Perhaps Brunetière is right: "Of all dramatic forms,
tragedy is the least realistic, in a sense the most symbolic, and,
as such, in its masterpieces, the least *contingent* or the closest
neighbor of absolute beauty." [1] In life, all seems at first sight to
be made up of contingencies. The curtain does not fall at a
climactic moment, we splutter occasionally in what should be
fine situations, bricks do break our heads at awkward and ridicu-
lous times, and more than once we are surprised by a *deus ex
machina* who liberates us without regard for artistic nicety. And
yet, for all this, the tragic idea, as it represents the search for
happiness by means or under conditions which themselves defeat that search, is one of the lasting and important ideas concerning human existence. From Leonidas in the Thermopylae
to Peter renouncing his Lord, from the heresiarch who burns for
a creed to the man who must choose between mother and wife,
the tragic idea reaffirms a particular phase of the stirring plati-
tude that "the world appears to be so constituted, that the
greatness of men leads only too easily to misery and ruin." [2] But
tragedy asserts more than "that men die and are not happy"; it
asserts that they die and are not happy through their own ef-

1 Brunetière, p. 152.
2 Volkelt, p. 91. The tragic fact in reality is discussed in our concluding
section.

23

forts. And not as a mere outcome of their own efforts, but *necessarily* as a condition contained in the effort. Tragedy, taken all in all, exposes an original and fatal defect in the relation between a purpose and a something within or without. Here we leave Aristotle to name the precise condition of downfall: *inevitability* impresses us as the kernel of the definition. No work can be tragic without it. Tragedy is always ironic, but it is not because an action *eventually* leads to the opposite of its intention, but because that opposite is grafted into the action from the very beginning. If this austere view of tragedy seems narrow, the pattern is nevertheless repeated time after time, in work after work. No other precise concept will bind the literature of so many years and so many nations together. The ironic idea that man's destruction can be occasioned by his very aspiration is obviously perennial and perennially fascinating, and it turns up in the guise of a thousand dramatic situations. The concrete applications of this idea—the plots which express it—are inexhaustible.

In naming inevitability as the *sine qua non* of tragedy, we do not discover something which had escaped the notice of critics these two thousand years; and indeed, it would be alarming had we done so. We are merely giving this concept the eminence which it has not achieved so far. Aristotle, for one, merely hints in our direction: "Thus a person of a given character should speak or act in a given way, by the rule either of necessity or of probability; just as this event should follow that by necessary or probable sequence. It is therefore evident that the unravelling of the plot, no less than the complication, must arise out of the plot itself, it must not be brought about by the *Deus ex Machina*." [3] Or again: reversal and recognition "should arise from the internal structure of the plot, so that what follows should be the necessary or probable result of the preceding action." [4] But Aristotle seems to be dealing here with the scenes or episodes of the play rather than, in all clarity, with the initial tragic purpose. Nor is inevitability at the center of his thoughts on tragedy. Still, if we feel the need for his authority, that authority

3 1454 a–b.
4 1452 a.

can be invoked from such passages as tending to support absolute inevitability at the very inception of the purpose.

In the work of contemporary critics too, the idea of finality occurs sporadically. It is not our purpose to catalogue authors and to parade allies, but a few critics may be cited here. Mr. Frye, for example, speaks of tragedy as residing "in the inevitability of the consequences of the [hero's] act, not in its moral significance as an act"; [5] Jaspers applies to tragedy his concept of the permanence along with the permanent limitation of the philosophic quest: "Man's mind fails and breaks down in the very wealth of its potentialities. Every one of these potentialities, as it becomes fulfilled, provokes and reaps disaster"; [6] while Miss Langer describes comedy as the image of Fortune, and tragedy as the image of Fate, by which she means that the latter, in abstracting the pattern of essential human behavior, shows man as aware of death and giving himself a career, a destiny, "shaped essentially in advance and only incidentally by chance happenings." [7]

Among the Romantic critics, the idea of inevitability assumed the more exalted names of Fate and Destiny. We dispense with these inflated terms at the risk of a certain dryness. The word inevitability is unevocative, but it has the advantage of "meaning business" and of being clear; and the still more important advantage of being suitable for any species of tragedy, whether Greek, Christian, atheistic, or merely secular.

5 Frye, p. 38.
6 Jaspers, p. 42.
7 Langer, p. 333.

5 · Paratragedies

THE APPLICATIONS of our definition of tragedy are so easily made, whether in plays or in novels, narrative poems or short stories, that a roll call of examples seems unnecessary at this point. The pattern recurs from the most rudimentary account of the sin and fall of Adam and Eve (as in Lydgate's *Fall of Princes*) to the decadent horror of *Das Schloss*; it is like a tune capable of infinite variations, yet always recoverable under the complications which the composers impose on it. It constitutes, if we love the word, an archetype; it is a theme behind themes. Armed with this concept, we separate tragedy from groups of other serious works—works of intrigue, works concerning passive victims, works of grave but successful action—which have often been enrolled in our category in the past; and we will apply to such works the term "paratragedy."

We have stated already that no definition can ever embrace *all* the works included in *all* other definitions. Still, we should avoid the parochialism which makes Frenchmen like Brunetière assert that there have been only two tragic periods: the Greek and the French; or the reply of Englishmen who assert that "twice only has tragedy flowered to full perfection, once in Periclean Athens and again in Elizabethan England." [1]

It will be useful to inspect a few works which we cannot admit among tragedies. *Oedipus at Colonus* is a moving story of redemption, with which we may class at once, though on a much lower rung, Tolstoy's *Resurrection*. Sophocles' *Electra* and

1 Dixon, p. 23.

Euripides' *Orestes* are dramas of just and successful revenge. *The Trojan Women* is a long lament. *Romeo and Juliet* may be called an idyll with an adventitiously melancholy ending.[2] The Renaissance in England and in Spain produced hundreds of bloody dramas of intrigue and counter-intrigue, plots, vengeances, ambitions and vicissitudes, ghosts, hideous criminals, and spotless victims, in all of which there is no question of a single purpose carrying from the beginning the necessity of the hero's undoing: I mention only Calderón's *El Mayor Monstruo los Celos* and *El Médico de su Honra*, Webster's *Duchess of Malfi* and *The White Devil*, Tourneur's *Atheist's Tragedy*, Lee's *Rival Queens*, and even Dryden's *All for Love*, which, though a superb play, has taken the tragic sting out of Shakespeare's story. For, where Shakespeare's Antony dooms himself by the very fact of his love when he "Claps on his sea wing, and like a doting mallard, Leaving the fight in height," flies after Cleopatra's sails, Dryden's hero oscillates between duty and Cleopatra, and in the end happens to be defeated in battle regardless of whether he leaves his queen or stays with her.

Calamities which befall through a dubious battle make a common type of paratragedy. Thus *Julius Caesar*—for, if Brutus had been victorious on the field, his conscience would have been quiet ("Did not great Julius bleed for justice' sake?" he asks as late as Act IV, Scene iii); thus Marlowe's *Edward II*, or Hauptmann's *Florian Geyer*. In none of these has the central purpose of the protagonists implied in its very being the overthrow that they suffer in battle.

Next we come to the stories of victims: heroes and heroines who perform little or nothing, who are therefore primarily patients rather than agents: in comic literature their prototype might be Dr. Primrose in *The Vicar of Wakefield* (with the cheerful chapter heading: "Fresh Calamities" for a motto). These are the persons whose fortune appears to depend entirely on the activities of others. We think of Aeschylus' *Agamemnon*, Euripides' *Andromache*, Goethe's *Egmont*, Schiller's *Don Car-*

---

2 I emphatically disagree with those who, seizing upon the expression "star-crossed lovers," make the catastrophe a cosmic concern, and see it as inevitable.

los (although there is a minor tragic incident in the play), Grillparzer's *Sappho*, Zola's *L'Assommoir*, Daudet's *Fromont Jeune et Risler Aîné*, Hudson's *Green Mansions*, Hemingway's *Farewell to Arms*, and others. In all these, we miss the purpose or action of a protagonist which logically entails his overthrow. Thus, the hero of Hemingway's novel is destroyed not by anything he himself does, but by the "accidental" death of Catherine in childbirth: an accident which expounds the very idea of the book, the "nada" of life, but which cannot be thought of as tragic. Thus too, in Grillparzer's play, Sappho is simply victimized by the fact that her lover changes his mind, falls in love with Melitta, and runs away with her.

Then we have enormous canvasses like Schiller's *Wallenstein*, which may have this or that tragic incident in them but are essentially chronicles; and finally the doomed purposes of unsympathetic persons or villains—Goethe's Clavigo, Hauptmann's Michael Kramer, Middleton's Beatrice (in *The Changeling*), and a crowd of others.

This list does not exhaust our rejections, of course, but it gives a few of the outstanding items. These works, needless to say, are not artistic failures; some, on the contrary, are masterpieces. But they do not dramatize what we call the tragic idea.

Let us make it clear that in the end it is not the word tragedy which matters, but the value of the category—whatever its name—which we have carved out. It is enough if the reader agrees that the concept as such, because it does in fact underlie so many works, because it unifies them, and because it is an important idea, deserves to be extracted and given a name. The most defensible name for this concept happens to be tragedy, for the simple reason that it covers a majority of the works hitherto so called. The category itself is significant—it is a fact of our civilization; the name is merely expedient.

A summary of a paratragedy from the repertory of "classical tragedies" may give a stronger idea of the ground for our rejections. One such work is Racine's *Mithridate*, an intrigue which happens to end happily, but might have done the reverse without changing its real nature.

The persons are Mithridate, King of Pontus; Monime, his betrothed; Pharnace and Xipharès, his sons by different mothers; and Arbate, his confidant.

Mithridate is reported dead. Young Xipharès—who, incidentally, hates Rome—aspires to the hand of Monime, promised to his father. So, however, does his half-brother Pharnace, who loves Rome. Monime complains to Xipharès of Pharnace's importunities; to his own declaration of love she responds modestly but with hints of reciprocation. She too hates Rome, and she hates Pharnace who loves Rome. News arrives that Mithridate is alive and about to return home. Pharnace, afraid of his father, proposes seizing the city; but loyal Xipharès refuses.

Mithridate appears, defeated by Rome, anxious for Monime, and suspicious of his sons. But Arbate (who favors Xipharès) impugns only Pharnace, accusing him of attempting to marry Monime. Mithridate angrily accuses Monime of trafficking with Pharnace, and calls, ironically, on Xipharès to argue Monime into obedience to him. Monime is unhappy, but she knows that she and Xipharès must separate forever. Xipharès, too, is distraught: "*Cours,*" he cries to himself, "*cours par un prompt trépas abréger ton supplice!*"—"Run, run, cut short your suffering by death!"

After various political matters, Mithridate accuses Pharnace (whose love for Rome he knows) of dallying with Monime. Pharnace counteraccuses Xipharès. Thereupon, Mithridate, much troubled, sets a trap for Monime: pretending to be angry with her for loving Pharnace, he bids her think no more of the traitor, but to marry Xipharès. She is overjoyed, and betrays herself.

Xipharès realizes that the game is up, and that Mithridate will kill him. Mithridate now plans to marry Monime: she, however, haughtily reproaches him for his outrageous trickery, and informs him that both she and Xipharès were overcoming their passion when the king surprised her. She leaves Mithridate undecided by this revelation whether to punish the two, or marry them. But on hearing that Pharnace has organized a rebellion, and the false tidings that Xipharès has joined him, he decides at any rate to kill Monime: *"Du malheur qui me presse Tu ne jouiras pas, infidèle princesse!"*—"You will not, unfaithful princess, enjoy my wretchedness."

While Pharnace's troops assault the palace, and fatally wound Mithridate, the latter sends a poisoned chalice to Monime. But then, discovering that Xipharès was on his side all the time, and that the young hero has defeated Pharnace, he recalls his order to Monime, and has her saved in the nick of time. He plunges a sword in his own breast, leaving the blissful Xipharès and Monime in each other's arms.

Mithridate, typical of hundreds of intrigue dramas of the Renaissance, is included in the canon of Racine's tragedies. But clearly it is no such thing. It is a serious play with a happy ending. If Monime had died, leaving Xipharès in despair, it would have been a serious play with an unhappy ending, but not one whit more tragic. The distinction between a work of intrigue and counterintrigue and a work in which doom attends the first hopeful movement of the hero is nothing less than radical.

6 · The Original Configuration

WE HAVE already seen that Aristotle speaks only incidentally of "necessity." When, in another place, he deprecates what he calls an "episodic" plot, he seems merely to be demanding unity of action—an action whose every scene is strictly relevant, and whose scenes cannot be shuffled about as can those, for example, of *Prometheus Bound*.[1] Nevertheless, as happens so often, the seed of the matter is there. We lose sight of inevitability in the Middle Ages, when the *Poetics* was not known, and when the very reverse of inevitability, namely the idea of fickle Fortune, was thought essential to tragedy. The French classicists no less than the Elizabethans and the Spaniards focused on the fall of the mighty without inquiring too closely into the fortuitousness or inevitability of the downfall in question. The German idealists, on the other hand, were more concerned with the metaphysic of the Absolute and its branches—freedom and necessity resolved into indifference, and so forth—to attend particularly to the form of plot. On the whole, though critics frequently praise the beauty or harmony of this or that example of inevitability, there is little evidence of a view that the difference between a *contingent* and a *necessary* downfall is so fundamental that it must be taken into account in a definition of tragedy. Indeed, in several modern works on tragedy, necessity is not even mentioned.

Why should contingent catastrophes, whether in the form of sheer accidents or of probabilities, be excluded from our defini-

1 See Else, pp. 325, 328.

31

tion? More than an exercise in semantics is involved. While the idea of inevitability does not force us into a distinct metaphysical camp, it does impose on the artist a peculiar handling of world phenomena by which his work acquires a momentousness denied to the other species.[2] By the same token, the idea creates for itself a unique form. The occasional surface resemblances between true and pseudo-tragedies may obscure this fact, but even a brief analysis suffices to separate the two species—to distinguish, say, between *Britannicus* and *Bérénice*, or between *The Duchess of Malfi* and *Othello*.

Where a particular idea logically involves a particular technique, an excursion into form may be the most instructive path to the concept behind it. Our goal, in this case, is to judge the meaning of the idea of inevitability, and to determine whether the distinction between episodic and necessary works is important enough to warrant a more refined definition of tragedy.

Inevitability is a concept partly of art and partly of life. Life offers us the model; it demonstrates that some actions by their very nature lead into an unintended calamity. But life tends to be a slovenly guide; and we can scarcely imagine a real situation in which some "way out" could not be found.[3] But what life presents as a strong or overwhelming likelihood, literature by its conventions makes a certainty. If we saw an Othello in actuality, we might hope that he had not quite succeeded in strangling Desdemona. And possibly Isabel Archer might go back to Rome only to find that Osmond had died of a stroke. But nothing shocks tragedy so much as the reversal of a trend— a reversal which is not, in its own language, necessary, and in the language of reality, overwhelmingly likely. It is the business of the author to organize a situation in which, artistically speaking, the chances of a happy resolution are nil. And this involves, on our part, an unconscious willingness to "play along."

We can appreciate this organization of experience best by thinking in terms of what may be called the *original configuration* of a tragedy. By original configuration is understood the total data, as given by the author, concerning the protagonist

2 Assuming, of course, that the work is not marred by other faults.
3 See, however, the concluding section for a discussion of "real" tragedy.

and the world as far as it is relevant to him, *at the moment of
the tragic action or decision.*

A tragic action or purpose taken out of its world, its context,
never carries in itself the cause of the actor's grief. Werther desires a married woman: why does he not obtain her? Emma
Bovary [4] longs for the perfect love affair: why is it impossible
that she should find it? Ahab wishes to kill a whale: why should
he fail? Oedipus looks for Laius' murderer: why should this
afflict him? Lord Jim jumps off a supposedly sinking ship and
saves himself: what makes him suffer?

We see that the drive, the purpose in itself reveals nothing to
us: certainly not how it should inevitably involve the protagonist's ruin. An action becomes tragic only in the completed
original configuration. The author, in other words, must furnish
the data which explain why the protagonist's quest is hopeless.
We say, then, that the overthrow of the protagonist appears
inevitable in the original configuration; that is, at the very time
of the tragic action. And the tragic fall can be defined as the
inevitable consequence of a given purpose *in a given world,* external or internal to the protagonist.

Now let us supply the data for the examples given above, by
which the otherwise floating purpose assumes its tragic weight.
Werther loves a married woman; does Goethe establish it for an
unquestioned fact that Charlotte will never run away from her
good husband? He does, of course. But why does not the in-
convenient husband die? Can we say that Werther's longing is
foredoomed, so long as we are not assured of Albert's immor-
tality? In the world of reality, we cannot. In reality we would
hasten to assure Werther that Albert could very well die, or
that some other accident might supervene and accomplish his
bliss. But the tragic writer eliminates mere possibilities from the
data which he organizes, and out of a *real* likelihood manufac-
tures the necessity of the work of art. And we willingly read as
though the unlikely were impossible; as though Albert could
not die or somehow vanish. It turns out that once we grasp the

---

4 *Madame Bovary* would be a perfect tragedy were it not for our uncertainty whether she "commands our good will." We use it here as an
illustration with this reservation in mind.

original configuration, we agree unconsciously to keep it fixed, to discuss it and nothing else, to lift it out of life and examine the consequences, the development, the unwinding of this pure situation according to the laws of reality. Accidents, in such a case, are by definition prevented from touching the isolated, central situation.

We shall deal again with accidents, and inquire how far they are permissible in this literature of inevitability. But let us return now to our full configurations. Why do we know that Emma's pursuit of ineffable love is vain? Because we accept Flaubert's given world, which is a vast *Homaiserie*. Given such a world—and the world is given again and again throughout the novel—Emma's endeavor appears hopeless. If we feel, while we read the book, that Emma could after all have found a suitable lover, that such things have been, that she had bad luck, etc., then we have misread Flaubert's data, or else must blame him for a failure. Actually, of course, he has not failed in the least. We do accept the world as he predicates it (though we can turn the next moment to *Romeo and Juliet* and adopt that world as well): we banish from our minds the possible accidents that might reverse Emma's fall at any point, and agree to deal in the archetypal world, where accidents cannot be; hence we *know* that Emma will not and cannot suddenly find her lover, or Homais turn into a Pasteur.[5]

We come now to the symbolic tragedy. No one thinks that it is impossible to kill a whale; but of course, the original configuration includes the whale's symbolic significance, which we accept without hesitation. We declare at once with Melville that the whale as given cannot be killed. Suddenly, having accepted this world, we pass from the tale of whaling to a tragedy. And again, given this configuration, we refuse to admit even as a possibility (for we have left life for art) a later accident that could destroy the configuration, and alter the theme. It is not possible (except in bad art) that the first mate should overrule Ahab, or that the boat should sink in a storm, for Melville has

5 Much the same remarks may be made about Chekhov's *The Three Sisters*, which also deals with a drive directed against a whole social climate.

isolated the essentials of the theme and must carry out his examination to the necessary end.

In symbolic tragedy it is desirable that there be as great a correspondence as possible between the symbol and the object. In other words, we ought to feel that it is "really" almost impossible to kill Moby Dick; and, in Ibsen, we should know that Solness "really" cannot stay up in the tower. Ibsen is entirely successful, for Solness' inability to endure high altitudes is firmly established—it is a part of the original configuration. Whether Melville's efforts—and they are not slight—to make the whale seem indestructible *in reality* are equally convincing is open to some doubt. In any event, where the literal nature of the symbol degenerates much further, the action becomes bloodless, and interesting as concept rather than as art.

Oedipus looks for Laius' murderer. The full configuration is very simple—he happens to be the murderer himself. Only by this fact, of course, is the purpose made tragic. Next, we remove all possibilities of averting the tragedy by untoward accidents, such as the death of an important witness, etc. For we wish to retain only the subject at hand—putting it crudely, that looking for a murderer when oneself is the murderer is a disastrous enterprise. Do we feel at any moment that Oedipus' inquiry was *not* necessarily fatal, because the shepherd might have been dumb in his grave? No; we have willingly removed ourselves from the world of rugged peculiarities: we are in a realm of statistical equipoise, safe from freaks.

In the case of *Lord Jim*, the original configuration consists of an inner ideal of courage shocked by a sudden overwhelming fear. We may observe that in these "inner" tragedies, the world of art seems to resemble the real world more closely; for the injury to one desire or value by the gratification of another is a very common real occurrence, and one that has relatively few essential elements. Nevertheless, this world is purged of accidentals, too. Lord Jim *cannot* suddenly shrug his shoulders and forget his cowardice: once we accept as a complete world his ideal of courage, and his leap off the boat, we obtain the pattern of necessary tragedy.

Necessity, then, is established in the most characteristic cases by the actual presentation to the reader of a complete pattern which includes the purpose and the co-existent elements which must balk it. Frequently, the author will underline the approach of doom by portents, mysterious predictions, visions, dreams, or natural warnings by fellow mortals. But he must be careful with these machines. Mere prediction by a hoary apparition, mere foreboding by a protagonist, will not make a misfortune which is not established in the original configuration seem necessary. Thus, the Chorus in T. S. Eliot's *Murder in the Cathedral*, though it forebodes Thomas Becket's death in eerie but unequivocal terms, does not establish the inevitability of that death; it but prepares us for an inevitability which will be made by the archbishop's own decision to seek martyrdom.[6]

As for *Romeo and Juliet*, generations of critics (and most ingeniously the Germans) have sanctioned it as an inevitable tragedy because of its atmosphere. "We obtain," goes a typical comment, "the impression . . . that in this world of hatred and of savagery, of folly and of senseless coincidence, so beautiful and so enraptured a love is necessarily doomed to defeat." [7] But though the lovers are indeed said to be "star-cross'd," it is difficult to admit that their downfall is really inevitable. Atmosphere, and a casual phrase, cannot do more than lend support to an objective fatality. *Romeo and Juliet*, like many a tale in Boccaccio, is a romance which, as the Restoration revisers realized, might have turned out happily as easily as otherwise.

In many, perhaps most cases, the original configuration is exposed from the outset, so that we may be immediately sure of calamity. But the author may prefer to withhold from the reader some part of the total configuration, just as he may withhold it from the actor himself. We watch the actor drink his cup, we see him fall and die, and only then realize that there had been poison in the cup. For one reason or another, it may suit the author to conceal the poison from us at the beginning. Thus neither we nor Orestes, in *The Choephori*, receive any inkling beforehand of the madness that must pursue him upon

6 For a discussion of the tragedy of renunciation, see Falk, *passim*.
7 Volkelt, p. 366.

his matricide. We know only of Apollo's behest to kill, which does not seem tragic, since Orestes is not moved (like his Euripidean brother) by any compunctions. Aeschylus conceals from us an important part of the original configuration—namely the moral order that forbids murder at the very moment Orestes raises his dagger. Therefore it is only when Clytemnestra and the Furies begin to bay that we realize how fatal was his act. In Tennyson's *Holy Grail*, the knights take a vow to pursue the Lord's cup:

> And Lancelot sware, and many among the Knights,
> And Gawain sware, and louder than the rest;

but it is only when Arthur returns that we hear how futile and damaging that action was:

> "Ah Galahad, Galahad," said the King, "for such
> As thou art is the vision, not for these."

We take a step away from pure tragedy when we are no longer quite sure that the original configuration involves the ruin that is to follow. An incident in Corneille's *Horace* will make this clear. We remember Horace as the inflexible Roman patriot who is ferociously ready and even eager to sacrifice anything he loves to his fatherland. He must fight Curiace, who is not only the brother of his wife, but also the lover of his sister Camille. Curiace is moved, but Horace does not wince: *"J'accepte aveuglément cette gloire avec joie."* [8] (II, ii.) So much is necessary for the understanding of Horace's character, which is the first feature in the configuration. By Act IV, Horace has killed the three Curiaces. Now that Camille's lover is dead, the unfortunate girl is expected to rejoice over the victory of Rome. Angered instead, she decides to make at least a final gesture to show her faithfulness to Curiace: she will proclaim her grief to Horace.

> *Loin d'éviter ses yeux, croissez à son aspect;*
> *Offensez sa victoire, irritez sa colère,*
> *Et prenez, s'il se peut, plaisir à lui déplaire.* [9] (IV, iv.)

8 "I accept this glory blindly, joyfully."

9 "Far from shunning him, rise up before him; insult his victory, chafe his anger; and take your pleasure in displeasing him."

When Horace enters, proud and triumphant, she taunts him and accuses him of brutality. Becoming incensed, he returns insults and tries to shame her. Finally, she invokes a terrible curse on Rome. Tension is high at this point, and the configuration is drawn. What reaction from Horace does Camille's invective, and her curse on Rome (Rome, his idol), demand? A blow, a great imprecation, or death? It is impossible to answer definitely, for all three ways are open, but only one can be called a great injury to Camille. Hence Camille's gesture is not necessarily fatal, though, as it happens, Horace leaps on her and kills her. His murder, in the light of the data given to us, appears as quite plausible (hence we accept the play), but not necessary. Corneille's failure has been his omission of some more distinct statement by Horace, or some action, to occur somewhere in the first three acts, which would have proved to us that if anyone— *anyone*, his wife and father included—had ever angered him on the subject of Rome, that person could not have escaped alive.

Nevertheless, *Horace* is at the very edge of tragedy, and Camille is so close to passing muster that one would prefer not to quibble. But another step, and then we face the unmistakable failures, where the author supplies the data, and insinuates that the protagonist's action or purpose was fatal in the world as given—yet fails to convince us. *We* see a way out where the author did not. *We*, at least, believe that the original configuration was by no means inauspicious. Edith Wharton's *Ethan Frome*, Pinero's *The Second Mrs. Tanqueray*, and virtually the whole body of Hardy's work in fiction can be cited as examples of *"tragédies manquées"*—attempts and failures to transcend the drama of intrigue.

If we turn now to the episodic paratragedy, we find that we are dealing with an altogether different artistic system. There are of course fine pseudo-tragedies, and a great many execrable tragedies; nevertheless, we will find that the pseudo-tragedy usually leaves something to be desired. It is the particular beauty of real tragedy that it strikes the reader's soul with fear from the onset, because the action is not subject to adventitious events. Tragedy presents the purpose and the world in which that purpose is born, and lets logic do the rest.

Thus it is no accident that Shakespeare's art reaches its climax when he progresses from the play of concatenation to the idea of inevitable catastrophe; and it is noteworthy that he stands well-nigh alone among the Elizabethans in his conscious or unconscious use of logical necessity. Without doubt, his grasp of this idea provides us with one of many clues to his universality. *Julius Caesar* appears at the threshold of the tragedies as a transitional play, looking back toward the episodic chronicles or the older revenge "tragedy" and forward to the remorse tragedy of *Macbeth*. In both *Caesar* and *Macbeth* a noble and trusted statesman murders his benefactor. In both plays, self-hatred is forecast in the very character of the protagonists. Unfortunately, while in *Macbeth* the spiritual overthrow is carried out, in *Julius Caesar* mind gives way to action. Brutus loses all his qualms the moment the deed is done. Caesar's apparition does not inspire, and was, indeed, not provoked by, remorse. The issue must then be decided by "chance" on the battlefield; but there was nothing in Brutus' crime which inherently promised war, and, if war, defeat.

We have already seen that battles usually make poor tragedies. We are never sure but the advantage might go the other way. To obtain tragedy, the author must withdraw all doubt from the issue: we must see a cursed Eteocles; the end must be certain from the moment of decision.

Accident, then, is an event which modifies the course of action implied in the original tragic configuration, whereby it appears that the protagonist's fate was not decided at the moment of his so-called tragic action.

A few examples from some minor works may be given. Lena, in Conrad's *Victory*, is ready to sacrifice her life in order to guard her benefactor's; and indeed, she braves all dangers for him, and has just saved him without injury to herself when a stray bullet kills her. Or Tolstoy's *Resurrection:* Nekhlyudov seduces Maslova, and thinks no more of her until years later when he happens to sit on a jury which is trying her for murder. Then remorse rushes upon him.

Familiar instances can be advanced easily enough, since almost the whole body of Elizabethan, Jacobean, and classical

Spanish drama can be classified as episodic drama. The pattern
in these works is plain enough. In all of them, the actors initiate
an action by which they eventually come to grief. But that
"eventually" works a momentous change from our concept of
tragedy. At the level of actual life, we have lost the vision of
implicit irony—the hope that carries in itself despair, the throw
that overthrows, purpose with the bar sinister of destiny. We
have lost Balzac's piece of shagreen, which taught us that to
will is to die, to go forward is to suffer.

In paratragedy our tension relaxes, our fear wanes, and frequently we grow angry because our hero need not have suffered
or died at all. The closed harmony of tragedy gives way to the
bustle of circumstances. We weave from doubt to hope, from
confidence to fear. The hero's purpose may or may not succeed:
this is the medieval world of Fortune—at any moment an external incident may turn his life upward or downward. The
protagonist is actually a victim, no matter how active he seems
to be, for ultimately it is not his action, his purpose which defeats him, but a more or less casual chain of circumstances
which it triggers. But tragedy shows the *inherent* flaw of the so-
hopeful purpose. The first action has logically decided the last.
The facile pleasures of the what-next have been removed from
us; we watch the gates close: before us is the man and his destiny, and nothing may come between them.

That's what's so handy about tragedy—you give it a little push so
it'll start rolling—nothing: a quick look at a girl passing in the
street who raises her arms, a yearning for honor one fine morning,
when you wake up, as though it were something to eat, one question
too many in the evening—that's all. After that, you just leave it
alone. You're calm. It rolls by itself. It's been punctiliously oiled
from the start.[10]

A distinct technique follows a distinct concept of art. True
tragedy is properly timeless or typical. Given the original configuration, and given the tragic purpose, it is a logical construction, erected with the pieces of reality, upon reality. Pseudo-
tragedy is, in one sense, a closer imitation of nature, for it denies
the logical simplicity of tragedy. It tells us that Charlotte may

10 Jean Anouilh, *Antigone*, Paris, 1946, p. 55 (my translation).

turn skeptic, and then she will no longer be the Charlotte that we postulated. In a deeper sense, however, pseudo-tragedy is further removed from reality: it can handle but one accident—life could offer a thousand different ones—and since the *one*, we can be sure, will never be repeated, we learn little in the end.

Thus, while we are often enough given to understand that tragedy has the quality of universality, we see that this universality, this timelessness, is due to a degree of abstraction, or simplification, which is predicated on the idea and technique of logical inevitability. We have seen, also, that this technique is in part an inspired artifact—a purification of nature for a better understanding of it, similar to that which is performed in controlled experiments in the laboratory. While pseudo-tragedy can be thrilling, and while it can excel in character portrayal, true tragedy is concerned with situations which can be regarded as generalized types of the human condition. And the test for a distinction between these two genres is in the presence of a dramatic purpose which is allowed to work itself out in the isolation of its context according to the inflexible laws of reality.

If we accept the view of tragedy just proposed, are we bound to say that the species must be austere and simple, that it bans all chance events? Actually, tragedy offers innumerable opportunities for accidents; its stage is often as bustling as that of an intrigue, so that we may be deceived into thinking the two are alike.[11] For instance, tragedy allows accidents before its beginning and after its end. We know that tragedies are not always coterminous with the works which contain them. Hence we do not object to any coincidence or extravagant accident which may precede or even create the tragic purpose. Not only must the author begin his work with some event for which he will show no cause, but he may very well start off with a *coup de foudre*, or something milder—a curious meeting, a dropped handkerchief, or an adventitious mistake.

More important, the post-tragic scene is likewise open to the author. It is here that he will introduce events which establish the final mood. Homais' success, Charles Bovary's discovery of his wife's past, and his death, are so many nonessentials which

11 For an able discussion of accident, see Henn, p. 23.

deepen the tone of despair. Milton, on the other hand, chooses to carry *Paradise Lost* beyond the tragedy in order to make a point of Christian hopefulness, and also to relieve the reader's dejection.

A second species of accident consists of contributory events. When a tragic author has set the purpose in motion, he may add a few accidentals to increase the tempo, accentuate the downfall, or vary the drama. It is of the essence that such accidents should not be decisive in any way. We may recall Faust's murder of Valentin; but even better are the accidentals which externalize and dramatize Margarete's inner disaster: the death of her mother, her drowning of the child, her imprisonment. None of these are actually implied in Margarete's sin; but neither are they the very stuff of her tragic suffering. Rather, they give dramatic emphasis to an internal debacle. Most tragedies of remorse are accompanied by these external marks. Indeed, as often as not, the very climax of the downfall is, strictly speaking, accidental. Oedipus' self-mutilation and Goriot's death, both contingent, end but do not constitute their tragedy. Most deaths, in fact, are not demanded by tragedy—as Racine recognized when he wrote *Bérénice*—but form its emotional climax.

The point is clear. Accidents are compatible with tragedy when they surround it, when they contribute to the necessary trend, when they climax or accelerate that trend. Through these accidents, too, the author can "individualize" without detracting from the generalness of the theme. We still know that given a certain personality and a certain world, young men like Werther must suffer. That their suffering should be increased here or tempered there, or that they should die or live on in the end, supplies so many modes of the unity, and gives the work of art its peculiar color.

7 · Prevented Tragedy

WHEN ACCIDENTS speed the action in the direction already laid down by the logic of the original configuration, they do not thwart the concept of tragedy. A tragedy is prevented, however, when the accidental event critically changes the direction of the supposedly necessary action. This is possible because the logic of inevitability is, ultimately, a fiction. A writer can always appeal to reality for even the most bizarre coincidence. He robs his work, to be sure, of the timelessness and purity which are the qualities of a literature based on the laws of likelihood. But this is not in every instance an injury to the work. We can only say that it changes the theme radically, and therefore removes that particular work into a very different category of serious art.

Interruptions may occur almost at any point of a work. Frequently we find the actor burdened with a purpose which is likely to prove fatal to him, but which, fortunately, he never has to put into execution. In Corneille's *Cinna*, for example, Cinna must kill the emperor if he is to retain Emilie's love—*"vers l'un ou vers l'autre il faut être perfide"*—"I must betray the one or the other." He actually comes to a tragic decision: namely, to kill Auguste; but then his rival Maxime reveals the whole plot to the emperor, and thus breaks Cinna's dilemma. At this point, of course, Cinna, from being a potential tragic hero, becomes a victim—but ultimately he is pardoned, and finds the reward of his very meagre virtue in Emilie's arms.

There are other examples of tragic purposes intercepted before they are fulfilled. One that deserves mention is Dorothea

Brooke's, in *Middlemarch*: here George Eliot guiltily (because inartistically) prevents a tragic dilemma from even arising. Old Casaubon, Dorothea's fogeyish husband, is about to extort from her an oath to continue his useless scholarly work after his death, and never to marry Will Ladislaw. The oath, which Dorothea is sure to take, will place her in a tragic situation. In order to prevent this, Eliot kills off Casaubon *just* before he has had time to hear Dorothea's promise.

Sometimes the nipping off does not comfort the hero. Agamemnon, in Euripides' *Iphigenia in Aulis*, must decide whether he will sacrifice his daughter or save her but face a war of all the Greeks against Argos. The dilemma does not come to a head, however, for Iphigenia suddenly makes her own free decision, and thus snatches tragedy away from Agamemnon. This hardly cheers the Argive, of course, since she still has to die.

Finally, in Thomas Corneille's *Timocrate* the queen has taken an oath that she will pursue Timocrate as long as she wears the crown. Timocrate turns out to be her savior and intended son-in-law. Here again, the dilemma comes to no action through her dazzling idea of renouncing the crown, and thus conjuring the oath away!

At other times, the tragic action has actually been initiated, or even completed; but an interference saves the hero from evil consequences. Is Neoptolemus' fall in Sophocles' *Philoctetes* realized when he decides to side with Philoctetes against Ulysses and the Greeks, seeing that Hercules intervenes almost at once to make the crooked straight? It is hard to tell in this case. Goethe's *Iphigenia in Tauris* provides a clearer instance. Iphigenia has decided to tell King Thoas the truth about Orestes' and Pylades' identity and their attempt to escape. She realizes to her horror that she has sacrificed her brother to virtue; but happily Thoas[1] proves to be amenable to the voice of romantic humanitarianism, and allows them all to leave his land.

Andromaque, we may remember, is in a somewhat similar quandary. In order to save her son Astyanax, she submits to a marriage with Pyrrhus which is abhorrent to her. The ceremony is performed, which is to say that the tragic decision is being

---

1 Like Mozart's Pasha in the *Abduction*.

carried out; but Oreste kills Pyrrhus, and thus Andromaque is saved.

The tale of Abraham and Isaac is a good prototype of the prevented tragedy: the decision made, the lifted sword, the sacrifice about to be consummated, and then the arresting voice of God which pacifies the soul. This story differs basically from tragedy *followed* by redemption as we find it in the lovely old tale of *Amis and Amiloun*.[2] Amis actually completes the sacrifice of his two children, and with great woe—

> For sorwe he sleynt oway biside,
> And wepe wið reweful chere.

His friend is saved as a result, but the price has been a bitter one. Only then comes the happy resolution, with the children found again. The difference, then, is plain. In the prevented tragedies, the hero may have suffered, and sometimes suffered gravely, but he has not had to act out his decision. If he has acted, then he has not had time to mourn. At one point or another, an intruder has modified the arrangement of purpose or action meeting necessarily with a grave suffering. Nevertheless, it must be conceded that the modification leaves a few works so close to tragedy that they are virtually indistinguishable from it.

2 For a discussion of post-tragic redemption, see section 21.

8 · Definitions by Ethical Direction

RETURNING to the definition of tragedy suggested by S. H. Butcher, we note again the phrase concerning the tragic hero: "through his ruin the disturbed order of the world is restored and the moral forces reassert their sway." Gilbert Murray, on the other hand, tells us that the dramatist "shows the beauty of human character fighting against fate and circumstance." Tragedy attests "the triumph of the human soul over suffering and disaster." [1] Here, succinctly, we read the two theses which still dominate the thinking of critics today, and which constitute definitions, or central portions of definitions, of tragedy. The first thesis is that tragedy is an assertion of cosmic justice; the second, that tragedy is an assertion of the greatness of man. Our own definition asserts neither the one nor the other; it allows cosmic justice and human greatness as suggestions or themes of individual tragedies, as it allows a multitude of other themes; but it does not allow these themes or suggestions to be quintessential.

That "Aristotle did not talk about art as an imitation of nature trying surreptitiously to convey the metaphysical 'Behind-nature'; that is, suggesting Big Ideas, or a Higher Reality, or a Concrete Universal or Absolute" [2]—so much is generally recognized today. One reason which has been proposed is that he could, after all, convey his sense of the divine order by means of a firm metaphysic and an equally firm ethic. Another

1 G. Murray, p. 66.
2 Ransom, p. 203.

is that he was not really very fond of literature. At any rate, he was properly corrected by later writers, who consistently demanded of art, and of tragedy in particular, a justification of the cosmic order. In the Middle Ages, the cosmic order was the Roman Catholic settlement of the universe. In the English Augustan age, the order which had to be justified was a more vaguely benevolent one. John Dennis was content to require that tragedy be "a very solemn Lecture, inculcating a particular Providence, and showing it plainly protecting the good, and chastizing the bad." [3] This may be naïve, but is it so different from the characteristic modern doctrine that "tragedy is at bottom man's most vehement protest against meaninglessness; . . . tragedy creates a pattern of human destiny in which man through suffering learns to live, not die"? [4]

If the requirement of piety—for piety is what we must call it, even in its contemporary disguise—is ageless, the other thesis, namely that of the beauty of human character and the dignity of man, can be traced back no further than to the Romantic age, when two conditions particularly favorable to this view obtained: the weakening of orthodox faith, leading men to a search elsewhere for consolations, and the revival of fervor as a virtue rather than a defect. This fervor, unable to satisfy itself in adulation of the Virgin Mary or divine mercy, turned to the creature man. Thus was born the apotheosis of Dante, Shakespeare and even Cervantes, and the new perception of tragedy as a vindication of human nobility. In the criticism of tragedy, this interpretation has persisted. The typical view is still that "great tragedy may rise from a ground of earthly pessimism, but it rises in the conviction of human worth and the divine splendour of things." [5]

Why did this view survive the Romantic age which had begotten it? The reason is obvious. From the early nineteenth century, a number of events too well known to require mention were alarmingly reducing the size of man. In our own day, glory has been shrunk to over-compensation, love to a tissue irritation,

3 Quoted in Muller, p. 5.
4 Weisinger, p. 230.
5 Bell, p. 15.

and honor to a weapon of the capitalistic bourgeoisie. "We can no longer tell tales of the fall of noble men because we do not believe that noble men exist." [6] The comforting suggestion that the point of tragedy is to show that man is *after all* a noble creature thus arose when men began to fear that he might after all *not* be a noble creature. As long as literary critics will be distressed by our loss of dignity, so long will they read the literature of the past as assertions of dignity. Such an imposition on the idea of tragedy did not occur to any critics living before the Romantic age: since they had never pictured man as a mere "bundle of reactions," they could not well be consoled by a demonstration that man was *not* such a bundle.

Where the requirement of a specific ethical direction— whether it be the thesis of justice or that of human dignity— is most vulnerable is in its subjectivity and in its historicity. This double weakness is worth examining here, both in the general definition of tragedy and in the evaluation of single works. Aristotle, as we have seen, does not directly concern himself with cosmic implications at all. The medievals, on the other hand, required tragedy to teach men the folly of worldly endeavor and material success, and the superior wisdom of turning one's eyes to heaven. Tragedy, for them, was a sermon. This view was still prevalent in Renaissance England. Thorndike cites Puttenham's definition (1589): "Tragedy deals with doleful falls of unfortunate and afflicted princes, for the purpose of reminding men of the mutability of fortune and of God's just punishment of a vicious life," [7] while Sidney mentions "the uncertainty of this world, and upon how weake foundations guilden roofs are builded." Against which we ought to set at once a scholar's understanding of the matter in our times: "The sovereign vindication of the artist is the exceeding beauty of all human vitalities, whether they are effective or ineffective, whether they succeed or fail. It is life as such that the artist loves: strong, exuberant, magnificent life, defying laws of

6 Krutch, p. 123.
7 Thorndike, p. 44. Are not the two ideas contradictory? In any event, this is Christian justice, not Hegelian or Bradleyan justice, nor the vaguer justice of modern critics.

time and space and conquering the impossible—circumscribed indeed, if we look at its scientific conditions, but absolutely free and untrammeled in its spiritual essence." [8] And after this, Hyllus' chant before the body of Heracles in *The Trachiniae:* "Lift him, followers! And grant me full forgiveness for this; but mark the great cruelty of the gods in the deeds that are being done. They beget children, they are hailed as fathers, and yet they can look upon such sufferings." [9] Does this allow for "exuberant life"? The glum note is to be sounded time and again in Shakespeare—"Our present business Is general woe," cries Albany in *Lear;* and "Graves only be men's works and death their gain! Sun, bide thy beams! Timon hath done his reign"— Timon's last words. As for Jacobean drama: "During the years immediately preceding and following *Lear* there was a distinct conception of tragedy as the representation not only of the depths of iniquity but of the moral confusion and blackness that beset us all." [10]

All this leads to Schopenhauer, who is also quite clear on what the vision of tragedy must be. The peculiarity of tragedy, he writes, is the "awakening of the knowledge that the world, life, can afford us no true pleasure, and consequently is not worthy of an attachment." [11]

To Joseph Wood Krutch, on the other hand, tragedy gives above all the impression that life is justified through the real nobility of heroes; while Dixon's opinion is that tragedy reveals a world of broken hearts and "heavenly creatures destroyed," after which reflections (such as Bradley's or Hegel's) concerning undying virtue and eternal justice are mere "comfortable speeches." [12] Nevertheless, the ultimate impression is of human souls "who do honour to our nature and give us hope for the world." [13] We wonder at the reader whose emotional reactions are nimble enough to suit this description. Campbell finds in

8 Courtney, p. 101.
9 R. C. Jebb's translation.
10 Thorndike, p. 169.
11 Schopenhauer, III, 213. This is half of the medieval concept shorn of its other half.
12 Dixon, p. 175.
13 *Ibid.*, p. 224.

Oedipus a sublimely reassuring view of life: "the noble spirit, if overclouded for a while by his own errors, conscious or unconscious, through the wrong-doing of others, or the inheritance of a burdened life, will in the end be vindicated or accepted of Heaven," [14] while Schelling is impressed by the felicitous fact that although necessity drives Oedipus to crime, free will makes him expiate, so that we are to obtain the effect of a beauteous reconciliation in the end. Fontenelle took away a different impression altogether: *"On ne remporte d'Oedipe et des pièces qui lui ressemblent, qu'une désagréable et inutile conviction des misères de la condition humaine."* [15]

Had Aristotle seen a performance of *Hamlet,* he would presumably have allowed the play to toss him to and fro between pity and fear, and noted in himself a sweet peacefulness in the end. A medieval Florentine clerk might have reflected on the vanity of this world, and the dangerous quirks of Dame Fortune. The English connoisseur of the early seventeenth century shuddered, we suppose, at the corruption of the world, or the calamitous degeneration of time. The French courtier, half a century later, could he have been prevailed upon to forgive Shakespeare his errors, would have seen in *Hamlet* an awful lesson about the consequence of vice, a lesson which would teach him to avoid the passions which plunged even so mighty a personage into misfortune.[16] The Johnsons of the eighteenth century left the theatre delighted with the "adherence to general nature" of the dramatist, his versatility, his justness of observation—and derived from Shakespeare sets of moral maxims! The idealist of the nineteenth century perceived the broken light of the Ab-

14 Campbell, p. 160.

15 "Oedipus, and plays which resemble it, produce only a disagreeable and useless conviction of the misery of the human condition." Fontenelle, sec. 49.

16 See Corneille, I, 53: "The pity which we feel when we see a misfortune strike our brothers leads us to fear a similar one for ourselves; this fear leads to a desire to avoid it; and this desire leads us to purge, moderate, rectify, and even uproot in us the passion which plunges the persons we pity into misfortune before our eyes." And Dacier, toward the end of the century, in his *Poétique d'Aristote:* "Tragedy, by exhibiting the faults which have brought these unhappy beings to misery, teaches us to beware of these faults, and to purge and moderate the passion which has been the sole cause of their undoing." Quoted in Robertson, pp. 377–78.

solute in Hamlet's aspirations, and felt convinced after the play that he had seen eternal free will struggling against necessity.[17] Schopenhauer and Hardy would have spoken of the folly of willing as the perfectly evident lesson of *Hamlet*, while Bradley *et alii* leave exhilarated by their vision of the greater power working toward justice. The writer, on rereading *Hamlet*, is impressed again with a sense of deep discouragement, immeasurable gloom: wanton gods shape the ends which we can only "rough-hew"—the world, in other words, is given over to a disorder in which plan and purpose are seldom answered by proportionate consequences; the virtue of Hamlet and Ophelia as much as the vice of Gertrude and Claudius run haphazard courses; hell and heaven dice for the upshot, and hell has loaded the dice. The lyrical end, the "good night, sweet prince," is a sad fluting of farewell by one who knows, though he himself is fortunate, that death is felicity.[18] But finally, a contemporary critic maintains of Hamlet that "we see him baffled by circumstance, but we are willing to witness that because we know that his nobility, the inner goodness of his being, will triumph over evil and over death." [19]

If we accept a definition according to structure or internal idea, we can use the word tragedy with enough lucidity to communicate among ourselves. But if a work is to convey a specific afterglow, an *a posteriori* message of gloom or of exuberance, of reconciliation or of mystery, in order to be a tragedy, the word must become useless. For few works of art have as their immediate theme cosmic justice, the nobility of man, or any other vision. These are "directions" presumably to be followed by the spectator in conjunction with the work, no matter what its subject or its apparent theme; even, it seems, with the multitude of

17 Not victoriously always; for Schlegel, the effect of *Hamlet* was "a maximum of despair" because it showed a permanent breach between man and Absolute Being.

18 Is such a view incompatible with "aesthetic satisfaction"? Obviously not. Does the beauty of the poetry subtly alter the mournful message? It does not. One of its tasks is to create the paradoxical state of mind in which a mournful message and joy cohabit, but never to alter the burden of the message.

19 Nicoll, p. 123. Easy profundity again. What is a dead man's triumph over death? Does Shakespeare propose a heavenly reward for Hamlet?

love-tragedies which have dominated the post-Hellenic scene. But we are left, then, with a welter of subjectivity. We are to ask of each person whether he really derives from *Hamlet* such or such a view of the cosmos, and perhaps to adjudge the title of tragedy only after a universal poll. We are also to shift the definition of tragedy from age to age, or else to suppose that only we, who have realized at last that the true effect of tragedy is to maintain against challenge the authentic stature of man, know what tragedy is.

Indeed, this last interpretation of tragedy, repeated though it may be at every opportunity nowadays, is so patently a local historical idea that its currency cannot fail to amaze. The vision of justice, at least, is venerable, for pious critics of all ages have tried to impose it on works however fractious;[20] though the meaning of justice has, needless to say, changed from one critical age to the next. But the idea of vindicated nobility could not emerge at any time prior to its first challenge; and that challenge did not come until the nineteenth century. Let us recall Sidney once more, for whom tragedy showed "the uncertainty of this world, and upon how weake foundations guilden roofs are builded." Is not this as authentic an interpretation of "the tragic vision" as the notion that tragedy expresses "the triumph over despair and . . . confidence in the value of human life"?[21] Sidney could never have received from a Senecan tragedy the refreshing notion of human nobility, for this notion was a presupposition of the age. Nor could the presupposition console him, for it was a mere habit. A hypothetical parallel of such a habit is not hard to find. An age of universal hunger might find it a consolation that the "hero" of *Death of a Salesman* ate three times a day. This fact does not, however, enter the con-

20 Critics tend to be more conservative and more conventional than artists, as is to be expected from the lower order of their genius. Artists with heretical tendencies must either ignore criticism altogether, like Byron, eventually surrender to it, like Tennyson, or, like Fielding, protest their pious aims with due vehemence and go their own way after all. How dull tragedy would be if artists, taking their cue from critics, felt obliged every time to exalt man and the cosmos.

21 Krutch, p. 123. The "nobility" theory can also be found in E. Hamilton's *Greek Way to Western Civilization* and M. Anderson's *Essence of Tragedy*.

scious or (one may venture to affirm) the subconscious mind of the modern spectator; neither are we consoled by the intelligence of Hamlet, though that is presupposed too.

The difficulty is that a work of art contains too many possible presuppositions, just as it contains too many possible visions. Bradley, for example, dwells on the impression of moral *waste* which we supposedly obtain from Shakespeare's tragedies. Evil, Bradley makes Shakespeare say, upsets the divine order which rules the world. The divinely ordered world therefore reacts violently against it. Unfortunately, the reaction is apt to be overimpetuous, and to involve the ruin of many good people as well. The order, then, is essentially just, but the tragedy is that its integrity "involves the waste of good." [22] Thus, in Shakespearean tragedy, the main action is "in greater or less degree, wrong or bad. The catastrophe is, in the main, the return of this action on the head of the agent. It is an example of justice." [23] Such justice will not allow us to be depressed or rebellious after witnessing the tragedy. Our vision is of a just yet mysteriously painful moral order, or, if we will, of a moral order mysteriously painful yet just.

Now the question which Bradley raises for us is whether the theodicy is *thematic* in Shakespeare—whether it is inherent in the very stuff of the plays—or whether it is only a possible construct erected on the plays. For, if it must be admitted that Shakespeare, unless it be in *Romeo and Juliet*, offers nothing in overt contradiction of this view, he offers nothing in overt contradiction to a dozen other views, including the simply opposite one.[24] For, if we had no Christian preconceptions, we might conclude that he depicts an essentially immoral order, a world managed by Satan. In this world Satan seizes upon one of God's favorites, and in one way or another, sometimes by sending a tool like Iago, or Lady Macbeth, or Cleopatra, sometimes creating a foul, corrupt, and sapping world like that of

22 Bradley, *Shakespearean Tragedy*, p. 37.
23 *Ibid.*, p. 31.
24 See Myers for a neoteric notion of justice which reconciles us even with *Romeo and Juliet*. The essence of tragedy, according to this author, is the perfect balance of pleasure and pain in the hero. Romeo dies, but he is reunited with Juliet. True, he is dead, but . . .

old Denmark, he hurls these favorites into sin, lets them damage and destroy as much virtue as possible, and does all this at the small expense of his tool. He destroys an Othello, a Desdemona—paragons of nature—and lets God smite his Iago. He leaves one or two minor kind souls to weep the beautiful dead heroes, and for a single Edmund or Claudius whom he abandons to destruction, carries off to Dis whole barrowfuls of slain innocents.[25]

This, in sum, constitutes the fallacy of "vision": reading *out of* a work, so to speak, an idea which can be logically inferred from it, but for which there is no literal warrant in the text itself; mistaking, in other words, an idea which is compatible with the text for one which inheres in it. Presuppositions, on the other hand, have the advantage of being undeniably warranted by the work: Hamlet *is* a noble man; his world *does* have several social classes. What then is our objection? Merely that presuppositions do no work in the text. They have no aesthetic function. The work of art is not about them. Thus, Hamlet's nobility of character is not offered in the text as a consolation, whereas Antony's, for example, is:

> The miserable change now at my end
> Lament nor sorrow at; but please your thoughts
> In feeding them with those my former fortunes
> Wherein I liv'd, the greatest prince o' the world,
> The noblest; and do now not basely die,
> Not cowardly put off my helmet to
> My countryman; a Roman by a Roman
> Valiantly vanquish'd.

25 In a newspaper article, Mr. W. H. Auden says of Shakespeare's plays that they convey "perfectly" his own favorite dogma that "we are all members one of another, mutually dependent and mutually responsible." (*The New York Times*, March 1, 1953.) It is of course true that such an idea can be derived from Shakespeare; it is also true that the same idea can be derived from almost every author who ever lived. Mr. Auden's point illustrates as clearly as possible the variety of interpretations which lie dormant, as it were, in every work of art, awaiting only to be awakened by a critic whose thinking happens to direct him to them. As I have suggested already, if we were to be engrossed for a week in the stupidity as well as the misfortunes of mankind, we might well write an eloquent monograph on "The redeeming intelligence of the Shakespearean heroes in their downfall."

Presuppositions do no work; "visions" are subjective. If aesthetics is to be a discipline, that is to say, a science of communicables, it must remain with the text at all times; it must deal with what is inherent and what functions, and not with the limitless world of possible deductions, inferences, and presuppositions which can be attached logically to the text, but which the text does not cope with. The critic must beware of his own cleverness, his excessively sharp eyes. *"Le plus grand défaut de la pénétration,"* says La Rochefoucauld, *"n'est pas de n'aller point jusqu'au bout, c'est de le passer"*—the greatest failure of insight is not falling short of the goal, but passing it.

9 · *Ethical Direction Inherent in the Work*

VISION, or ethical direction, is not a portion of any meaningful definition of tragedy. On the one hand, any given statement leaves out of account too many works which otherwise qualify as tragic; on the other, it surrenders the category to the anarchy of subjective or historical interpretation, of which we have tried to give a sample in the previous section. All this does not mean, however, that a tragedy does not, or should not, say anything about the universe. Quite to the contrary, the proposed definition seeks to liberate our conception of tragedy so that we can entertain any number of themes, some of them mutually incompatible, but all of them referable to our master concept. For the latter, as we have already noted, describes a fundamental human situation which can serve a variety of metaphysical schemes and an even greater variety of concrete "plots." We are not by any means suggesting, then, that tragedy, or literature in general, is an "hypothetical verbal structure" whose only relation to the real world consists in its taking materials from the latter in order to erect its own arbitrary, though pleasing, word structure. Tragedy is acceptable only on condition of being in some manner true to the world which supplies it with materials.

An idea about man and the universe can be more than a merely possible inference from a tragic work. Frequently, it appears as the very essence of the work, turning the latter into an avowed *Weltanschauungstragödie*. A *Weltanschauungstragödie*, however, does not necessarily neutralize a further, independent aftervision, since it is not likely to pronounce on every possible philosophical, social, or psychological issue. In Hardy's novels, for example, we are not allowed to gain an impression that there is even a remote world justice. But Hardy does not denigrate his protagonists, and we may sense in these novels an attitude of respect before the human being. This may, but also may not, relieve our gloom in the end, for we can dwell on the futility as well as on the joy of being noble. What matters is that no one in these novels, nor Hardy himself, preaches—even in the subtlest, most "artistic" manner—on this subject. No one says, even in the subtlest indirection, that the world may be ruled by the doomsters, but at least Henchard was a great man. If someone did say this, every reader would find that the gloom had been partly dissipated. As it is, the consolation is just allowable, because not denied by the text, but it can hardly be required of the reader.

Thus, the tragedy which offers, say, a vision of the nobility of man must do so more or less explicitly. The greatness of Prometheus, of Polyeucte, of Ahab is the very stuff of the tragedies in which they appear. But whereas Hamlet and Lear are indeed noble, their nobility is not offered by the poet as a theme. Such, then, is the distinction between ethical direction as possible aftereffect and ethical direction as theme.

The "world-view" of a work, as against a mere interpretation, does not have to be trumpeted in order to be audible. It may be suggested more than stated. Synge's *Riders to the Sea*, for example, rises irresistibly and yet most subtly beyond its own brief facts. Note the "widening" effect of Maurya's final litany:

Maurya: They're all together this time, and the end is come. May the Almighty God have mercy on Bartley's soul, and on Michael's soul, and on the souls of Sheamus and Patch, and Stephen and Shawn (*bending her head*); and may He have mercy on my soul, Nora, and on the soul of every one is left living in the world.

It is touches like these which expand the scope of a work of art, and unquestionably cast great shadows behind the actors and the actions, until they not only remain themselves, but become the delegates of universal powers. It is suggestion, but suggestion in the text.

In short, although no one idea is bound to arise out of tragedy, concerning God or the ways of the universe, or the relation of man to man, we are by no means free to derive any idea from any work. Further, if the very theme of certain tragedies is cosmic in scope, others refuse themselves to any grandiose interpretation whatever. Shakespeare seems to dramatize no universal scheme at all, which means in his case (as we know by sad experience) that every ambitious critic can apply his own. The French classical dramatists are notoriously flat, not to say shallow. Even in a *Polyeucte*, even in an *Athalie*, it seems as though the dramatists had never perceived the vastness behind a moral or theological point. *Andromaque* stubbornly remains in its own small world. But beginning with the romantic revival, men turned again to art as to an oracle, and *Faust*, *The Brothers Karamazov*, *Moby Dick*, *Das Schloss*, to name but these, convey undeniable metaphysical theses; while on the socio-political side, there have appeared another group of resonant tragedies, from Balzac and Ibsen to Malraux and Silone.

Of course, we cannot be forced to obey the directions suggested by our authors, but if we fail to accept their "verdict," we are at odds with the works themselves, and our judgment becomes idiosyncratic. Chaucer's *Troilus and Criseyde* ends in heaven, where the wronged hero, contemplating the world and his own overthrow, muses complacently on the inanity of mortal longings. Only an idiosyncratic judgment will be consoled by the notion that virtue triumphs over death, or depressed by a vision of immortal chaos. Only an idiosyncratic temperament will leave the poem in a state of deep gloom. The text demands a certain response, it dictates an intellectual and emotional aftereffect.

In *Prometheus*—an extreme example of joy in tragedy—the great god cries out his triumph even as he suffers. His choice has more of good than bad in it. His pain is amply compensated for by his exhilaration. There is no one in the play who makes a sardonic response to Prometheus' chant; there is no subtle counterpoint of doubt, no final question mark. The text *orders* a triumphant mood; only a senseless eccentricity would gainsay the author. Grillparzer's *Medea* is at the opposite extreme. Not a gleam of light penetrates here. Medea, abandoned by her husband, feared and rejected by her children, banished by the

king, dejectedly revenges herself, but she ends as gloomily as she
began:

> *Was ist der Erde Glück?—Ein Schatten!*
> *Was ist der Erde Ruhm?—Ein Traum!*

Erde Ruhm?—Ein Traum!
"What is joy on earth?" she cries. "A shadow. What is re-
nown on earth? A dream!"

The comments on the world by Hardy's characters are well
known. Swinburne's Althea and Meleager hate God and the
universe—

> seeing in death
> There is no comfort and none aftergrowth.

However we turn the matter, these writers represent the cosmos
as basically evil or indifferent, not by a merely permissive aftervision, but thematically. For middle cases, in which the protagonist sets a theme neither joyous nor despairing, we may cite
Synge's *Deirdre of the Sorrows.* "I have put away sorrow like a
shoe that is worn out and muddy, for it is I have had a life that
will be envied by great companies." This is from Deirdre's
speech-before-last, and suggests a kind of consolation which
neither Hamlet, Lear, nor Othello provide. Antony too, as we
have seen, dies in such a way that we are compelled to moderate
our grief.

Sometimes it is not the mood or utterance of the actor which
determines the ethical direction, but some plain speaking by
the author himself, the remarks of subsidiary actors who know,
the more difficult-to-define atmosphere, or the appearance of
certain meaningful symbols. But whether or not a work broadens
out at all beyond its obvious data can itself be a legitimate point
of contention. One man may read into a speech a suggestion of
hope or despair which another does not perceive. But the principle is clear. For the theme of a tragedy, we must read the
lines, not between them.

The multiplicity of world views allowed by the proposed
definition enables us to dispose of that new version of the Quarrel of the Ancients and the Moderns, namely whether modern
tragedy is possible. Rationally posed, the question is one of
definition: is tragedy a work which exhibits or presupposes an

absolute system of values, true nobility of character, cosmic justice, or the possibility of free will? If all or any of these are postulated in the definition, it must be admitted that modern tragedy can (at best) be written today only by reconfirmed Christians. But our own definition, which rejects the necessity for any of these doctrines,[1] easily admits contemporary tragedy.

The distinction between high and naturalistic tragedy is a useful one, just as useful as that between Periclean and Elizabethan tragedy; but it belongs in a history of tragedy rather than in a definition. The tragic concept demands only a purpose of some magnitude in the hero and his capacity to arouse our good will. True, an artist who denies the possibility of either will not be able to produce a tragedy. (*Waiting for Godot* comes to mind as a masterful example.) But naturalism—or modern literature in general—allows for both in its own modest way. Indeed, the protagonists of *Germinal*, of *Man's Hope*, and of *The Old Man and the Sea* have an all-but-epic grandeur about them; they are recent avatars of the epic spirit. But even the humbler Mrs. Alving, with all her twentieth-century descendants, fits simply and naturally into the tragic standard. Our definition provides for modern tragedy, hence for the continuity of the tradition, without doing violence to the importance of the tragic idea.

Every age which imposes its own pet doctrines on the theory of tragedy finds itself forced into critical acrobatics. In the seventeenth century, no degree of obvious effectiveness in a play could make it palatable to the critics if it violated the *a priori* rules—or shibboleths—squeezed out of Aristotle. Today, convinced that only free will or absolute grandeur of soul can make a work tragic, critics will reject the most clearly successful works and relegate them to some inferior class.[2] It is a curious question why every generation finds it necessary to denigrate

1 For a discussion of free will, see sections 15–16.
2 For a minor but striking example, see Arestad, *passim*. The author, having convinced himself that successful tragedy requires free choice and a world of real values, and that *Ghosts* has neither, somersaults into the absurdity of favoring *Brand* and *Emperor and Galilean* over it. In the same way, Shakespeare for the classical age was not good because according to the rules he *could* not be good.

itself in favor of the past. Should not our own age, so conscious of history, have been proof against this silliness? For the contention that we have no tragedy is far more than a semantic quibble; it means, properly translated, that we have lost the glory, that we have become second-rate.

That the idea of tragedy has accommodated itself to the grey flannel suit and even to Bermuda shorts shows, if anything, the vitality of modern art—its refusal to become ossified by a tradition. But the abandonment of heroics here is no more drastic than that of the gods; the conceptual distance between Chekhov and Shakespeare no greater than that between Shakespeare and Aeschylus.[3] The tragic idea survived the loss of the gods and it survived the loss of the aristocratic hero. It adapts itself to the thought and the ethos of every age—to the Greek pantheon and the goddess Themis, to Christianity, to feudalism, to sentimental deism, to social humanitarianism, to materialistic skepticism, to communism, to existentialism.[4] The human situation—that to strive is to stumble, that we undo ourselves by doing, that volition is flawed at the core—the fundamental irony of existence, which is more important than any creed, subsists behind all creeds. In this light, it will surely seem arbitrary in a critic to draw a line and say "Here tragedy ends."

3 Or between Aeschylus and Euripides. To Aristophanes it seemed that the work of Euripides, with its domestic squabbles and "small consciences," constituted a collapse from the heroic standards of Aeschylus. The battle of Ancients versus Moderns can be played within fifty years, if need be.

4 See Krieger, *passim*, for an able definition of existentialist tragedy.

10 · The Emotional Effects of Tragedy

OUR DEFINITION of tragedy dispenses with Aristotle's requirement that it arouse and then eliminate pity and fear. The oddity of this requirement is exceeded only by the strangeness of the flood of commentary it has caused these two thousand years. There can be little objection today to keeping it out of the definition. But we will go further, and disallow *any* given emotional consequence as a requisite for tragedy. Tragedy is an idea. Like any other idea, it is certain to arouse emotions in mankind. But as with any other idea, these emotions will vary. We shall take it as an axiom that no idea inherently arouses a specific emotion. It follows that the idea of tragedy cannot be charged with one.

Further, a fact which has not been noticed often enough is that definitions which demand a response of pity or fear with or without their purgation, or emotions such as awe, exuberance, terror, admiration, rule out of the domain of tragedy all bad art.[1] For obviously, no bad work of art can produce any of these emotions. This is an absurd state of affairs. Does a sonnet cease to be a sonnet because a poetaster has made it? Does a house cease to be a house if we do not live in it? Does a murder cease to be a murder if we are not shocked by it? In short, we cannot define our term by some function which it ought to fulfill in its perfect state. If we do so, we must coin another term

1 See, however, McCollom, who accepts the honorific association of the word as a part of its definition. "Among other traits, tragedy has the character of marked effectiveness" (p. 3).

for all the "tragedies" that fail to move us as we desire. In order to keep our term stable whatever the quality of the work, we must eliminate pity, fear, admiration, and all the rest from our basic definition.[2]

Like the definition by ethical direction, the definition by emotional effect leads to the most confusing subjectivity and historicity. Are we to watch our emotions as we read or sit at the spectacle, and if we do not observe pity and fear in ourselves, decide that the work is not tragic? Or must heads be counted, and if more than half the critics are moved, must the work be judged a tragedy? And if in one age the tragedies of a former time are no longer the fashion, and no longer move the audience, do they cease to be tragedies? Few readers bred to Shakespeare are likely to feel anything like pity and fear at the reading of Corneille and even Racine: are these therefore not tragic authors? And can a work be tragic in France, and not in England? Furthermore, must it arouse pity *and* fear, as Aristotle seems to require in his casual manner? The Renaissance called on admiration and wonder as well. The seventeenth century underscored fear: terrified by the hero's fall, the spectators were to quell dangerous passions in their own souls after leaving the theatre. But the humane eighteenth century trusted man, not believing, like Bossuet, that he needed to be frightened into being good. Goodness was natural to man. All tragedy had to do was to draw it out by exhibiting pitiful spectacles.[3] When Schiller came to define tragedy in the last decade of the century, he omitted fear altogether.[4]

The whole argument reduces itself to this: if tragedy is to

2 At the same time, we will agree with Lessing that the unforgivable sin in a dramatic author is "to leave us cold." But this is the unforgivable sin in every artist, in every medium. Schiller, in his definition of tragedy, describes it as having the *intention* of arousing our pity (pp. 197–98). This at any rate allows for works whose intention was not matched by their success.

3 This shift was concomitant, as Wasserman points out, with that from the aristocratic (fearsome) to the bourgeois (likeable) hero.

4 He was preceded by Lessing, who, in interpreting Aristotle, conjured the notion of fear away by making it a portion of compassion—"fear is compassion referred back to ourselves" (No. 75)—and then defining tragedy as "a poem which excites compassion." (No. 77.)

be defined, even in part, by a response in the reader or the spectator—a response, that is, of the kind which changes like a Proteus from age to age, from person to person, from nation to nation, within one person even from period to period—then the term becomes useless as a description of a work of art; for it gives to each reader a private range of objects which happen to elicit the required response at a given time in his life. To say, then, that tragedy is a fiction affecting the reader with emotion x or perception y is no better than to define a dwelling as a structure which gives feelings of security to him who sees it, by which definition a lifeboat might be a house, but Bluebeard's castle would need another name.

Aristotle, of course, required not only that emotions be aroused, but also that they be purged. Purgation has been interpreted in various ways. The seventeenth century took it to mean that the spectators got rid of impediments to virtue; Herder and other critics, that they lost impediments to reason; what Aristotle himself meant has never been established, but it is hard to see that it matters very much. The most familiar adaptation of his doctrine to the requirements of the twentieth century is that of I. A. Richards. Catharsis, says Richards, is a reconciliation into a state of repose of opposing impulses. "What clearer instance of the 'balance or reconciliation of opposites and discordant qualities' can be found than Tragedy? Pity, the impulse to approach, and Terror, the impulse to retreat, are brought in Tragedy to a reconciliation which they find nowhere else, and with them who knows what other allied groups of equally discordant impulses." Through "their union in an ordered single response" we find release, restoration, repose, balance, composure; and that is catharsis.[5] This reconciliation implies, incidentally, that the writer must not "sublimate" the ugly facts of life. Where other critics *demand* a revelation of order and justice or a compensatory heaven, Richards will not even permit it, for this suppresses one of the opposing impulses.

Another modern theory is even more frankly therapeutic than that of Aristotle or Richards. "The essential function of Trag-

5 Richards, p. 245.

edy," writes a critic, "would appear to be the complicating and strengthening of the psyche by means of shocks from the outside: not, of course, violent and disorganizing shocks, but mild, preventive, reorganizing ones." [6] We gain power to meet the real shocks of life through our attendance at the playhouse just as a soldier who frankly and vividly anticipates the horrors of battle is less liable to suffer from shell shock than one who conceals the event from his own consciousness.

Still another writer emphasizes the gratification of opposing instincts, though in terms somewhat different from Richards'. Tragedy is said to give authority to "our most urgent and stubborn—and *therefore* most strongly resisted—desires" while at the same time we are gratified by the punishment of the hero.[7] Desire and inhibition, the id and the superego, engage in mock battle to the rapt satisfaction of the witnessing ego.

Are these notions fantasies? Or do they really report correctly what takes place in all, or a few, people? A skeptic might suggest that they will vanish without trace in a few years. Whatever the answer may be, the point for us is that they have no place among the requirements of tragedy. They cannot be members of the definition on the grounds already offered. Tragedy, in our estimation, must be tragedy even to the quiet soul whose superego lives in perfect concord with the id, or to the person who is incapable of pity.

This much said, we may legitimately inquire into human experience for a few hints concerning the actual range of emotion covered by tragedy. A distinction must be made of course between specific emotions (with or without their purgation) and the ultimate impression of pleasure which draws the spectator to the source of these emotions.[8] Thus, pity and fear are one thing; and the paradoxical pleasure which we derive from experiencing them under the condition of art is another.

We will not be grieved if the following examination of

6 Morrell, p. 26.

7 Lesser, p. 133. This theory seems to do for the individual what Miss Bodkin does for the race.

8 The feeling of pleasure is the subject of the next section.

emotions does not correspond with every reader's experience. Our intention is to explore and to illustrate the astonishing range of possibilities.

What then are the impressions we might obtain from *Prometheus Bound, King Lear, Bérénice, Atala, The Mill on the Floss, Wuthering Heights, Ghosts, Atalanta in Calydon, Portrait of a Lady, Einsame Menschen, Deirdre of the Sorrows,* and *La Porte Etroite?* It is self-evident that the lighter emotions are not going to be invoked here. But aside from this, such works are often more widely separated from each other than from certain nontragedies. If we saw *Prometheus Bound* and Sophocles' *Electra* performed one after the other, we should feel within ourselves two fairly similar states, even though *Electra* is not tragic at all; whereas *Prometheus Bound* followed by *Deirdre of the Sorrows* would have nothing closer in common than an impression of deep and grave satisfaction.

That all the works we have listed realize the tragic idea is evident. In *The Mill on the Floss* Maggie gives way to a fatal impulse, and runs off with her cousin's lover, thus transgressing her own ideal of moral rectitude at terrifying cost to herself. In *Ghosts,* a mother tries to conceal and efface all traces of her vile husband, hopefully yet all the time vainly, for her very son has inherited a terrible disease from his father. Althea, in *Atalanta,* kills her own son to avenge her brother, and sinks in utter despair. The categorical imperative calls once more in *Portrait of a Lady,* when Isabel sacrifices her happiness at the behest of a higher duty. Hauptmann, grappling with a similar situation, makes his Johannes Vockerat renounce the happy life with Anna in order to remain with his wife; a decision so intolerable that he commits suicide in the end. Deirdre chooses the horror of death in order not to grow old and forget what love is.

In every case, the protagonist, in order to obtain something desired, inevitably involves himself in great suffering. Yet we respond all along the prism of emotions. Triumph, remorse, despair, resolution, horror, indignation, resignation, submission, melancholy, or a mixture of many in the protagonists call forth the same wealth in us. Compare Prometheus' cry—

> Let the whirling blasts of Necessity
> Seize on my body and hurl it
> Down to the darkness of Tartarus—
> Yet all he shall not destroy me!

—with that of Hyllus in the *Trachiniae*,[9] or the excruciating farewell of Oedipus to his children. Or contrast it with the tearful despair with which Chateaubriand's *Atala* closes: "*Ainsi passe sur la terre tout ce qui fut bon, vertueux, sensible! Homme, tu n'es qu'un songe rapide, un rêve douloureux; tu n'existes que par le malheur: tu n'es quelque chose que par la tristesse de ton âme et l'éternelle mélancolie de ta pensée!*"[10] Whereas the gloom of Swinburne is healthy and dry-eyed and lyrical:

> the night gathers me,
> And in the night shall no man gather fruit.

In contrast again, *Portrait of a Lady* makes hardly more than an emotional ripple. Isabel is staunch and determined, and just a little bleak; her triumph has not the exuberance of Prometheus', even though in both we feel that there is more gained than lost. *Ghosts*, again, ends with a harshness into which the final lyric vociferation bursts with staggering effect. Whereas *The Mill on the Floss* weeps bourgeois tears and leaves us unconvinced. The emotional impact of *Einsame Menschen* is the terrified feeling of being trapped. *Deirdre* is all singing melancholy: "It is a cold place I must go to be with you, Maisi; and it's cold your arms will be this night that were warm about my neck so often. . . ." And yet she ends her life with these words: "It's a pitiful thing, Conchubor, you have done, this night in Emain; yet a thing will be a joy and triumph to the ends of life and time."

And what emotion has *Deirdre* in common with *Bérénice*?

9 See p. 49.
10 "So passes on earth all that was kind, virtuous, sensitive! Man, you are but a swift and painful dream; you exist only by misery: you are something only by virtue of your soul's sadness and your thought's eternal melancholy!"

Deirdre is an ineffable play, and it engenders a constellation of emotions. Racine's tragedy is elegant, lucid, declamatory. In the fourth act, Titus, still wrought upon by his illegal passion for Bérénice, declaims to her:

> *Je sens que sans vous je ne saurais plus vivre,*
> *Que mon coeur de moi-même est prêt à s'éloigner;*
> *Mais il ne s'agit plus de vivre, il faut régner.* [11]

Pity? Fear? Perhaps for the seventeenth-century courtier. We, for our part, observe that Titus indulges in wit at the crisis of his life. What has he in common with Lear?

> And my poor fool is hang'd! No, no, no life!
> Why should a dog, a horse, a rat, have life,
> And thou no breath at all? Thou'lt come no
>   more,
> Never, never, never, never, never!
> Pray you, undo this button: thank you, sir.

Or this stunning despair with the contracted, hothouse atmosphere of *La Porte Etroite*, in which a futile piety ends in nothing, no thing gained, only loss and ruin;—the almost intolerable insistence of Alissa on the narrow gate and yet her desperate love for Jérôme: *"Seigneur! nous avancer vers vous, Jérôme et moi, l'un avec l'autre, l'un par l'autre. . . . Mais non! la route que vous nous enseignez, Seigneur, est une route étroite —étroite à n'y pouvoir marcher deux de profil."* [12]

And what, finally, is the emotional connection between the intellectual daylight power of *Ghosts* with the heath and heathen furies of the night at Wuthering Heights?

Except insofar as all good serious literature provides for us an "aesthetic satisfaction," tragedy does not come attended by one or two specifiable and necessary emotions, nor necessarily by discordance or reconciliation, tension or integration. This should be obvious from the immense variety of subject matter

---

11 "I feel that without you I can no longer live, that my heart is ready to part with myself; but living does not matter; I must reign."

12 "Lord! to advance toward you, Jerome and I, one with the other, one by means of the other. . . . But oh! the way you teach us, Lord, is a narrow way—so narrow that two going side by side cannot walk on it."

and forms represented in tragedies. Some tragedies are in prose, others in poetry, good or bad. Some are narrow, personal in scope, others dramatize cosmic forces. Sometimes the mood is violent, sometimes lyrical, sometimes muted. The griefs may be short and deadly, or long-protracted. A reconciliation may soften the end or the protagonist may fall darkly into darkness. In short, the tragic idea is pliable: it yields to a thousand fingerings. The complexity of our emotional state at the conclusion of a work, and the great number of different possible complexities, make it impossible, in the end, to agree with any critic who undertakes to inform us in a few, striking words, what emotional effect tragedy shall produce. From tragedy that crushes to tragedy that exhilarates a gamut not merely of single notes can be struck, but an endless number of chords. And finally, we include as well bad, boring tragedies which, aside from boredom or irritation, make no perceptible impression at all. The recognition of the idea of tragedy can be perfectly blank.

11 · *From Pain to Pleasure*

ONE OF THE OLDEST questions in art criticism is why we are amused by the spectacle of pain. While this question assumes a particular pertinence in the drama—where we may be accused of seeking the same thrill which was experienced by the crowds at Tyburn or the *tricoteuses* during the Terror—it arises also in other forms of literature, including the lyric poem, and in other arts, namely the dance, the graphic and plastic arts, and even in music. It is obvious that the experience of pleasure and pain does not arise from the spectacle of pleasure and pain respectively; that pain in spectacle may give pleasure, and that pleasure in spectacle may give at least a kind of pain, usually that of boredom. This phenomenon has a great interest for the moralist. It seems to attest to a certain backwardness or savagery in the human race. The perfect human being would feel disgust not only in the face of actual evil, but also at its representation, unless (as, say, in the Crucifixion) the latter divulged something noble or hopeful about man. This does not mean that he would shun such a representation, for he would seek it in the interest of truth; but he would not experience what we call "aesthetic satisfaction" in the spectacle. He would be instructed, but horrified. Even in our less-than-perfect era we see variations among people which tend to support this view. Some persons, by no means pathological cases, enjoy executions; others are repelled by executions but enjoy bullfights; others are repelled by bullfights but enjoy the rawest brutality in the film; others are repelled by such brutality but enjoy farcical pratfalls; and some are repelled even by farcical pain and can enjoy only a representation of evil which seems to have a purpose. Is it mere fantasy to imagine a state of mind—again, not pathological—which would discover no pleasure in *Oedipus* or in *Hamlet,* not because of insensitivity, but on the contrary because of perfect nobility?

Actually, it has sometimes been denied that the spectacle of pain brings pleasure. The fall of a perfect man, at any rate, could only arouse disgust, Aristotle erroneously supposed. What, then, was one supposed to do if the theatre *demanded* perfect heroes? This problem faced the French dramatists of the great age. Fashion required perfect virtue on the stage, but it believed that the fall of perfect virtue was not only morally inadmissible, but also, on the simple psychological level, unpleasant. The result was the *tragédie heureuse* (surely the most bizarre coinage of literary history), in which poetic justice is strictly accomplished: the paragon of virtue overcomes the danger at the last moment, and the villains are punished. It is worth quoting Corneille on this subject in full:

> *En effet, il est certain que nous ne saurions voir un honnête homme sur notre théâtre sans lui souhaiter de la prospérité, et nous fâcher de ses infortunes. Cela fait que quand il en demeure accablé, nous sortons avec chagrin, et remportons une espèce d'indignation contre l'auteur et les acteurs; mais quand l'événement remplit nos souhaits, et que la vertu y est couronnée, nous sortons avec pleine joie, et remportons une entière satisfaction de l'ouvrage, et de ceux qui l'ont représenté.*[1]

Racine's theory is equally positive. "*Quelle apparence,*" he exclaims in the Preface to *Iphigénie,* "*que j'eusse souillé la scène par le meurtre horrible d'une personne aussi vertueuse et aussi aimable qu'il fallait représenter Iphigénie?*"[2] And when he

1 "Indeed, it is certain that we cannot see a good man on our stage without wishing him prosperity, and grieving over his misfortunes. As a result, when the latter cast him down, we are pained, and carry away a kind of indignation against author and actors; but when the outcome fulfills our wishes, and virtue is crowned, we go away full of joy, entirely gratified by the work and by those who have staged it." Corneille, I, 21.

2 "Is it likely that I should have tarnished the stage with the horrible murder of a person like Iphigenia, who must be presented as both virtuous and lovable?" Racine, I, 688.

fortunately violated this precept, as he did, for example, in the death of Hippolytus, he disingenuously contended that Hippolytus had a weakness which made his death palatable, namely his love for Aricie. We are not concerned here, however, with the subterfuges by which French dramatists occasionally evaded their naïve doctrine. Enough for us to take note, without stooping to a refutation, of the doctrine itself, that there is no pleasure for the spectator in the spectacle of arrant injustice.

Why as a matter of fact do the educated Western man and woman find pleasure in "painful" art? We cannot hope to arrive at a pristinely new solution of this problem, but an inspection of the major answers given in the past—and most of them still current—may at least enable us to choose among them more sensibly:

A] Those who interpret tragedy in terms of an assertion of the nobility of man or the justice of the universe are of course in possession of a ready answer. If "tragedy occurs when the accepted order of things is fundamentally questioned only to be the more triumphantly reaffirmed," [3] if tragedy is "a fiction in which pain is fitted into a plot that gives it meaning," [4] if tragedy exhibits "the triumph of the human soul over suffering and disaster," [5] then our pleasure derives inevitably from the reaffirmation, the meaning, the triumph, whatever other sources it may be indebted to besides. This is naturally true also of any other affirmation which is said to reside in the very being of tragedy. For Schiller, to use but one example, tragedy exhibits *"die Macht des Sittengesetzes"*—the power of the moral law; pain procures us an agreeable emotion insofar as it is a condition of the triumph of morality—when, say, the protagonist renounces a pleasure for a duty, or when the guilty hero suffers remorse. "The experience of the victorious power of the moral law," Schiller asserts, " . . . is so high, so real a good, that we are even tempted to be reconciled to evil, which we have to thank for it." [6] Actually, the visions of *ultimate* justice, virtue, or

3 Weisinger, p. 266.
4 Pottle, p. 629.
5 G. Murray, p. 66.
6 Schiller, p. 175.

order, with which we have occupied ourselves so much in the course of this essay, are only a notch less naïve, even at their most modern, than the old demand for poetic justice.[7] Poetic justice requires the material triumph of virtue; finer minds are content with the spiritual triumph. Virtue is only *apparently* defeated. Man's spirit soars in all its glory above the misery it has endured. But this, rightly considered, is only poetic justice at one remove, and the pleasure which it generates is almost as simple as that which occurs when the gods snatch Iphigenia—or Isaac—away to safety. We remain with the problem of why pleasure occurs when the redeeming vision is not present, or at least not experienced.

In terms of our own definition, which neither demands nor precludes a moral affirmation, it must be allowed that where such an affirmation is made, it will undoubtedly contribute to our well-being and joy; but *only* contribute, for no assertion of nobility can redeem, say, Dryden's heroic plays from their dreariness. Our moral exaltation is triggered, as it were, by an aesthetic satisfaction which is (within limits) independent of it. Once permitted and released, it joins with this satisfaction and multiplies it, the two becoming a kind of compound in which the elements can no longer be separated. This exaltation is properly peculiar. We leave the theatre or rise from our reading with a kind of inebriation in which all our faculties are pushed into the direction of supreme acceptance.

The most common type of tragedy in which this exaltation is generated is, naturally enough, the tragedy of dilemma, where the protagonist must choose between a greater and a lesser good—usually the ethical against what Kierkegaard calls the aesthetic. *Prometheus* is the prototype of this species of tragedy. The protagonist chooses the nobler part and suffers or dies. In a

---

7 This is well illustrated in the work of Herder. Herder demands a reconciliation with fatality which will purify our emotions at the end of the play; he is not so naïve as to require simple poetic justice. Yet he expresses the need for this subtler kind of "happy ending" almost in the same terms as do Corneille and Racine: "We weep bitter tears enough in life . . . ; whoever makes it the aim of his art to impress on us this daily misery, and to embitter the cup of life without medication, is no artist, but a poisoner, or an ignorant apothecary." And he adds that the noble tragic hero should be a guiding light for us (p. 383 and *passim*).

modern work, he may bitterly regret his nobility; but traditionally he meets his doom with considerable *brio;* and his euphoria normally communicates itself to the spectator. Such then is the role which moral affirmation can play. It helps us to explain our satisfaction with certain works of art, but the mystery of pleasure in painful art remains unsolved.

B] When Aristotle mentions the purgation of pity and fear, we may suppose that he had in mind too the pleasure which comes of this kind of relief. But whether he spoke as a physician, as a moralist, or as a political theorist—whether he desired the expulsion of these emotions for hygienic, ethical, or civic reasons—he does not seem to have been particularly interested in the pleasurable consequence of a cure. Neither, after all, would a doctor, priest, or statesman today introduce this "subjective element" in his analysis. But if tragedy, or any work of art, really effects a purgation, our problem is solved. In modern terms—those of I. A. Richards and his followers—we have been treated for our discordant emotions, our inner conflicts. Pleasure, as Richards remarks, is simply the by-product of the treatment. We have been strengthened; we are ready to take on life; "we suffer an ordeal," says a post-Richards writer, "face life at its most difficult and complex, but derive pleasure in the new readiness and power we have gained thereby." [8] Is this view very different from that, already quoted, of Corneille and Dacier to the effect that tragedy will induce us to repress unconstructive drives and to become better adjusted to the demands of reality? (I have translated from seventeenth- to twentieth-century jargon.) Three centuries ago catharsis was interpreted as the elimination of bad passions; today it is as an insurance for sanity. But neo-classical virtue is really mental health in an older idiom. We will allow ourselves to be as skeptical of the one as of the other, and to doubt, on the one hand, whether anyone's virtue was amended by *Andromaque* in the seventeenth century, and whether any psyches have been strengthened by *Ghosts* in ours.

C] The argument that our pleasure derives from malice

8 Morrell, p. 29.

(*Schadenfreude*) has been often refuted and deserves no further comment.

D] The opposite argument, that we take pleasure in the act of sympathy, is more plausible. It became a favorite solution in the eighteenth century, the age of sensibility, when an apparently untapped source of joy was discovered in the "gentle affections":

> 'Tis woven in the world's great plan,
> And fixed by Heaven's decree,
> That all the true delights of man
> Should spring from Sympathy.[9]

In our own century, Thorndike has spoken of the "self-congratulation that comes with the exercise of sympathy," [10] a view which goes back, honorably enough, to Castelvetro. The exercise of sympathy need not be bound to any self-congratulation, however, and it should be allowed an independent claim. Nor is it precisely the same thing as pity. The theory seems to claim that we enjoy so much loving Desdemona that we will endure her suffering and our pity for the sake of that pleasure. Wasserman quotes an eighteenth-century critic: "Virtue, ever lovely, while labouring under distress appears with a double lustre.—Constrained by its attractions, we run to the theatre, and embrace objects of distress, notwithstanding the pain they afford us." [11] Pity, as Spinoza remarked, is a positive pain, but perhaps we suffer it willingly in order to be exposed to the lovable emotion of love.

However attractive this theory may be—and we admit its strength—it clearly does not cover the whole case. It does not explain, for example, our inclination for *danger* in tragedy. Surely the appeal of danger is not that it enhances the lustre of virtue; it gives us a separate thrill; as does, indeed, the emotion of hate, and even that of indignation. We do not reject the theory, then, but we wish to supplement it.

---

9 Cowper, quoted in Wasserman, p. 297. I am indebted to this article for its fine account of pleasure theories up to the Romantic period.
10 Thorndike, p. 17.
11 Wasserman, p. 285.

E] "Our exultation in the death of Hamlet is related in direct line of descent to the religious exultation felt by the primitive group that made sacrifice of the divine king or sacred animal, the representative of the tribal life, and, by the communion of its shed blood, felt that life strengthened and renewed." [12] We have already declared our incompetence to cope with the tribalizing views of art. If these atavistic exultations dwell in our consciousness, we are forced to demur, in company with all others who, upon an honest inquiry into their own minds, have failed to discover a tribal joy. If they are in the unconscious, we will allow them to remain there, and beg of them not to disturb our quest for the communicable.

F] "The function of tragedy," says F. L. Lucas, "is simply and solely to give a certain sort of pleasure, to satisfy in certain ways our love both of beauty and of truth, of truth to life and about it." [13] This is perhaps not a very instructive passage, but we may retain in it the notion of truth to life, and associate with it—I do not know how legitimately—Aristotle's assertion that we derive pleasure from imitation. It is the fashion nowadays to deride the "message" of a work of art. "The beauty of the patterns of poetry lies within poetry and is self-justifying," we are told. [14] To which the older reply is that the pattern is justified in part by the "truth" of its relation to the real world. [15] The instruction which the reader or spectator has traditionally been thought to derive from works of art may well give enough pleasure to compensate for the pain he feels because of the hero's suffering. Such instruction need not be obvious by any means. It does not necessarily depend on a set piece of *dianoia*. The interplay of character, the characters themselves, the moral life of the work, the actions and reactions, the themes stated and implied—all these are satisfying, not as arbitrary non-Euclidean creations, nor merely because they satisfy our curiosity for the what-next, but because they hit truths, whether these truths be light or dark, and whether we knew these truths

12 Bodkin, p. 21.
13 Lucas, p. 51.
14 Pottle, p. 641.
15 For a discussion of this controversy, see the author's "Sources of Value in Poetry," *Centennial Review*, III (Spring 1959), 212–23.

before or not. This is not a naïve plea for "realistic" art. The strangeness of art is that Aeschylus and Congreve, Zola and Kafka, each in his manner, feels his way—or so *we* feel—to a truth. So much is obvious. But we are pleased not only when the truth is told, but also, knowing it already, when it is retold. Our pleasure is often one of recognition. The priceless scene in Shakespeare's *Troilus and Cressida* in which Cressida and Pandarus witness the parade of Trojans may not tell us anything new about women; but at least it reminds us; it restates; it brings something we possess to life again. In this enlarged sense, instruction, even in things painful, is a source of pleasure.[16] But once more, the pleasure occurs *despite* suffering, not because of it.

G] The work of art—we speak again of any art, not of tragedy only—discloses the power of an artist, which in turn elicits our admiration. Once more we seem to be given here a compensation for pain, rather than a pleasure *in* pain. But the claims of this theory are worth our consideration. Perhaps the classic statement is in the first part of the following by Hume (the second part we shall deal with in our next division):

The genius required to paint objects in a lively manner, the art employed in collecting all the pathetic circumstances, the judgment displayed in disposing them: the exercise, I say, of these noble talents, together with the force of expression, and beauty of oratorical numbers, diffuse the highest satisfaction on the audience, and excite the most delightful movements.[17]

And a more recent statement: "We never discover in the work a single evidence of technique, discipline, deliberation, without having the value enhanced further." [18] How far admiration of the author's skill goes toward compensating us for our pity and terror, and how much it counts in the complex of feelings which we call aesthetic satisfaction, it is hard to say. We have already seen that the portrayal of pain may please us inasmuch as it is

16 If interpretation of reality gives pleasure, so, it must be added, does "instruction" in what reality should be (e.g., idyllic art) or in what reality might descend to if —— (e.g., anti-Utopias).

17 Hume, p. 261.

18 Ransom, p. 209. See also Smart, p. 36.

instructive. We may also exclaim at the skill with which it is brought into the picture, the intelligence with which it is rendered—the genius of a particular word or of the special moment at which the word is said. Such a reaction, if it takes place, does not animate us side by side with the others; undoubtedly it loses itself in the compound. Common experience allows that it does exist as a reaction; that we do say, "Ah, the man was a master!" as well as, "It is a great work." We know, too, that we crave originality, and that a work loses its value if it is shown to be plagiarized. "It is always a pleasure to talk with an intelligent man," someone says in *Karamazov*. The sense of conversation with genius is a permanent delight. How else shall we explain the need so many men have felt to ascribe the *Iliad* to a single poet, or to enhance his genius by giving him the *Odyssey* as well?

H] The second part of Hume's statement deals with beauty; only we take it in the larger sense to include all the formal elements (including diction) which enter into successful composition. What then is the relation of beauty in this large sense to the pain of tragedy?

In the first place, the whole problem could again be solved simply by denying the painfulness of a situation when it is skillfully used in the work of art. We are once more in the world of "hypothetical verbal structures," in which Desdemona's death is comparable to a red horizontal in Mondrian: a portion of the "geometry" of this particular structure. We will be pained if the event does not, for example, conform to the inner logic premised by the work; but we are not to grieve because we would grieve were it occurring in reality.

Unfortunately, the case is not so simple. We are more likely to resemble Dr. Johnson, who touchingly admitted "I was many years ago so shocked by Cordelia's death, that I know not whether I ever endured again to read the last scenes of the play till I undertook to revise them as an editor." For most readers, then, even today, a painful episode is not transubstantiated into joy because it is an artifact. We feel Cordelia's death as real pain—a pain no different in kind at least from that which we should experience before a real event. And the paradox still remains that we seek out this pain.

Others assert that the beauty of the work covertly moderates the pain. The poetry of *Hamlet,* for example, alters the theme of chaos or corruption at the core of the play. How can a universe be thought foul in which such poetry is spoken? By the same token, *Madame Bovary* as work of art is a perennial parallel rejoinder to the pessimism of its thesis. The logical consequence of this view is that the only truly pessimistic work is the bad one. In order to create an impression of an evil universe one would have to write not only a "sad" but also a defective book. But this is mere confusion. The joy we feel over the poetry of *Hamlet* does not alter our intellectual vision. Chaos remains chaos whether it is expressed in sonorous poetry or in Dogberry slang. We must deal separately with these two questions: first, whether there is hope for the human race; and second, whether the work of art expresses hope for the human race. We are free to say that as long as a *Lear* or a *Metamorphosis* can still be written, our glory is still ours; but our conclusion has no right to slink back into the work to alter its own avowed pessimism.[19]

A third possibility is that, while the pain remains pain, as Johnson's remark seems to indicate, we return to the work because of the beauty which exists side by side with it. The appeal of Racine's rhetoric and of the structure of *Ghosts* is such that we willingly endure what is painful there, suffering the wound for the sake of the blessing—blessing of form as well as of vision. However, this solution is only partly satisfactory. When we are conscious of beauty as an operating influence, we feel that it exerts an effect on the painful event itself. Beauty may—we go no further—it may palliate the pain itself.

This then is our solution. Hamlet's world is not less terrible because of the poetry, but poetry may make us know it without nausea. We apprehend the pain but do not suffer it, or at least

19 Thus, when Flaubert and Malraux speak of art as the only possible victory of man in a futile and senseless world, they are referring to art's place in the world, not to the world's place in art.

do not suffer it so much. Where beauty is imposed upon a
painful scene, or upon a painful thesis, it acts as an interposi-
tion; it absorbs part of the shock; or, to change the figure, it
sends a cooling stream to mix with the scalding one. We still
know the true temperature, but we have lost the pain of this
knowledge. This is not to deny in the least the independent joy
we take in beauty, a joy which may, indeed, operate simply as
compensation for the calamity. Our theory considers only the
effect of beauty on the painful event itself.

This leaves us, however, with Dr. Johnson on our hands. Evi-
dently beauty can in certain cases fail to palliate the horror of
an event. Not a few readers reject the ablation of Gloucester's
eyes, or the mutilations in Faulkner, for all the poetry or formal
beauty with which these are invested. For the separation between art and reality is an invention of critics. It breaks down
repeatedly in actual experience, and satanic content may neutralize perfect form.

1]   "Le coeur," says Fontenelle, "aime naturellement à être
remué." [20] This doctrine, founded on Descartes, was popular in
the seventeenth century. [21] The eighteenth, as we have seen,
adapted it to its own prejudices by adding a qualifying phrase:
moved, but especially by the tender emotions. But this destroyed the validity of the original statement, which strikes us
still as the most reasonable explanation for the pleasure we take
in the representation of calamitous events.

The fact is that we do not need compensations for the painful
events in tragedy: we had rather be moved by pain than not
be moved at all. Man is the only animal capable of boredom,
the only animal that cannot spend energy as other species do, in
random movement. He is agitated by passions which only the

20 "The heart by its nature likes to be stirred." Quoted in Wasserman,
p. 290.

21 Descartes perceived the power of "unpleasant" objects to give
pleasure, and vice versa. We take pleasure in all kinds of emotions on the
stage, "even in sadness and hatred," because we enjoy vicarious emotions.
"Reading of strange adventures in a book, or seeing them enacted in a
theatre, arouses in us sometimes sadness, sometimes joy, or love, or
hatred . . . ; but with all that, we like to have these stirred in us, and this
pleasure is an intellectual joy which can be born of sadness as well as of all
the other emotions." Les Passions de l'âme, Art. 94, 147.

passion of fear holds in check. Civilization subdues his actions, but it does not rid him of the desires. He is eager for change and for adventure; he likes repose only after exertion; he is naturally curious, and wants to try, to finger, to sample. But he learns that change is often cruel, and adventure dangerous. In the social contract he disarms his neighbor, but at the cost of being disarmed himself. He surrenders to an unnatural *stasis*—livened here and there by a quarrel with his wife, an increase in his salary, or one drink too many. He craves the great emotions which, when twice or three times they do come to him, turn out too painful after all. Where will he find the emotion without the pain? The answer is, in art; pulp fiction for the vulgar, Henry James for the "elect."

Art gives us the adventure and withholds the pain; exercises our emotions but allays their discomfort; arouses fear without danger, pity without injury, love without responsibility, defeat without humiliation, luxury without work, power without effort. With art, we can even feel what it is to die, without dying.

This is no magic key to the secret of art. We are dealing with one more reason why the spectacle of pain does not produce the sensation of pain; but this expatiation of our emotions, this indulgence after long confinement appears as the most plausible, or the most general of the reasons which we have surveyed: the love of agitation for its own sake, without an exact discrimination between pain and pleasure. "The fullness of life," says Tieck, "a healthy, strong feeling of existence [*Dasein*], requires even a certain degree of mourning so as to experience delight [*die Lust*] more intimately." [22]

All writers have added here what we have already implied: the condition that this agitation must be safe. The most famous pronouncement is that of Lucretius:

> It is sweet, when on the great sea the winds trouble its waters, to behold from land another's deep distress; not that it is a pleasure and delight that any should be afflicted, but because it is sweet to see from what evils you are yourself exempt. It is sweet also to look upon the mighty struggles of war arrayed along the plains without sharing yourself in the danger. [23]

22 Quoted in Mann, p. 39.
23 *De Rerum Natura*, II, 1–6. Munro's translation.

Johnson is not the only witness to the fact that the painfulness depicted in a work of art can leap out, as it were, and make us smart as the real world is wont to do. One of the functions of form in art (and by form we may understand here all the devices of diction and structure by virtue of which the work is an artifact) is to create that sense of distance which is a condition of psychological safety—just as physical distance from danger is a condition of actual safety in life. Pain breaks through and hurts instead of pleasing when these artificial screens fail. We cannot, of course, predict such a failure by a consideration of the work of art in itself, for it depends also on the history of the viewer. But it is not difficult to state the general conditions under which this failure may occur. The more vulnerable we as audience are to a given source of pain, the more novelist or playwright will have to resort to "distance-making devices"—complex structure, symbolism, ancient or remote settings, poetry, etc.— in order to keep us with him. No wonder, then, that many people today, to give but one example, avoid films concerning the last war;—the same people, indeed, who will see and enjoy the same horrors provided they are dressed in ancient uniforms. Such is the danger of "modern" and "realistic" art, and, conversely, the advantage (exploited by the Greek, Elizabethan, and French dramatists alike) of the remote and the ancient.

Have we got here a clue to the strange fact that the pseudo-tragedies which deal with sheer victims rather than with purposeful heroes are especially liable to break through the artifice and give us real pain? Hegel has already deprecated "misfortune merely as misfortune," holding that "such pictures of lamentation and misery merely rack the feelings," and demanding that tragic suffering be "suspended over active characters entirely as the consequence of their own act." [24] Arnold, in the preface to his poems in 1853, gave as an excuse for the withdrawal of *Empedocles* that "no poetical enjoyment can be derived" from situations "in which the suffering finds no vent in action; in which a continuous state of mental distress is prolonged, unrelieved by incident, hope, or resistance; in which there is

24 Hegel, p. 300.

everything to be endured, nothing to be done." Now we are not concerned here with the conceptual distinction which removes such works from the realm of tragedy. We note only that such works are far more often painful than are genuine tragedies. It is the Euripides of the *Trojan Women* who was the most pathetic of the Greeks. But in actuality too, we are far more deeply affected by the death of an innocent victim than by that of an agent.

What mechanism is at work here? In our terms, the art which concerns itself with Desdemonas is more often painful than that which deals with Othellos. It hauls us out of our safety, in despite of form. Were the reason simply that victims are pure while the tragic heroes have a flaw, the psychological situation would present no problem. Aristotle seems to have been aware of the fact that the suffering of a perfect character might be psychologically (and not only morally) intolerable. But the truth of the matter is that the overthrow of a flawless hero is still less painful than that of an imperfect victim. Perhaps—we offer this with great caution—the audience feels obscurely, in the case of the active hero, a satisfaction which is akin to the satisfaction of justice, though actually no real justice occurs. The hero suffers *because* he tried. This is not far from saying that he *paid* for trying, unfair though the term may be in all objectivity; not far from saying that he *invited* disaster.

But perhaps an even better explanation is that with the man who suffers or dies as a result of his own action, we feel that we are safe, for we can (and usually do) choose not to imitate him. "He died trying to conquer Everest; well now, here is something *I* shall never be doing, but how thrilling to watch!" Whereas anyone can be a victim: who knows when somebody will point a gun at me, or creep into my house at dead of night? The victim is trapped, unaware, helpless, and these are the things we dread most. We all hope to avoid being fools like Lear, but how can we avoid being Cordelia, who is struck unawares by another's crime and folly?

We have touched on two—and only two—common conditions which are unfavorable to the sense of pleasure which we seek even in painful art: excessive realism or modernity, and the depiction of victims. More than once we have drawn on instances from the actual world. It is worth stressing that just as, in the broadest way, aesthetic satisfaction is a composite largely made up of emotions which are aroused by reality (the imitated thing), so in regard to the particular problem of pleasure-in-pain, the laws governing our reactions apply to actuality as much as they do to art. The words of Lucretius which I have quoted, and which are always used by literary critics, refer to reality. In reality, too, we can distinguish between the pain which does and that which does not ruffle us according to the thickness of the screen between ourselves and the event. Let us consider four stages of painful experience:

1] The pain happens to me. For example, I become sick; my son is a failure; my wife loses her sister. The "I" obviously takes in all those who are so close to me that their feelings are immediately mirrored in mine. At this stage, pain is most truly pain.

2] Lucretius-like, I witness a riot from my balcony, and feel a certain excitement, a well-being; I am all attention; I have a sense of being godlike. But then a man is killed under my eyes; he looks up toward me and stretches out his hands, then falls over in his own blood. My excitement is dissolved in pity.

3] I pay money and go out of my way to see the newsreel of a "tragic" event—say, a shipwreck. Mothers cry out, lifeboats are upset, men vanish in the dark. My eyes are full of tears, but "I wouldn't have missed the newsreel for the world." If *my* mother had been among the victims, I could not have borne it.

4] I read with excitement an account of Attila's atrocities, but cannot endure to read the diary of a girl who eventually perished in a German concentration camp.

It seems, then, that the best explanation for our acceptance of pain in tragedy, namely that we love agitation within limits, applies to reality as well as to its "imitation." The form of a work of art does not absolve it from the laws of reality. It makes easier the detachment which we require, but it does not insure detachment. Art is but one more removal from *me*, but it is only a matter of greater distance, not a removal to another realm in which other laws—the laws of aesthetics—operate. We accept pain in a work of art when it serves the harmony of the work as such; when it tells or retells a truth; when it is diminished by the beauty of the artist's workmanship; when it points to some good beyond. But we more than accept it; we look for it, because we love to ventilate our passions in safety. The passage to avoidance and flight comes, as it does in reality, at the moment when pain becomes pain-for-me; and this passage can occur in any work of art, the best and the worst. For art is not a discrete reality. It is creation, but also interpretation. It is something new, but not quite new.

In sum, asking only why it is we take pleasure in the spectacle of pain (and ignoring the question of aesthetic satisfaction at large), the reply, we find, is complex. The pain of fiction is sometimes experienced as pain by the spectator, and sometimes it is diminished and sometimes it is transformed. When it is felt as pain, it may be accepted because it is compensated for; or it may be rejected so violently that the work of art itself falls. And when it is transformed, it functions as pleasure because we seek relief from *stasis*.

12 · A Stable Definition

THE IDEAL of criticism is to approach the condition of a pure science—that is to say, to characterize, estimate, or classify by means of stable and permanent criteria. Science exists as science by virtue of two stabilities: one of the object under investigation, the other of the investigating subject. This is speaking ideally, of course, since the subject, for example, is not so reliable but he is compelled to repeat his experiments and his observations a number of times, and to arrive at a mean result. But setting aside minor difficulties of this kind, we still find the dual stability which makes possible what is called accuracy, and which enables man to communicate and to predict.

Stability in the subject is obtained by relying exclusively on human faculties which experience shows to be analogous to the point of identity in the whole race, known deviants excepted. By these faculties we understand chiefly the senses. If the human retina were "temperamental," or if it "progressed" from one age to the next, science would become impossible, communication would cease, and each man would be, to an extent undreamed of by the poet, "in the sea of life enisled." [1]

By stability in the object, we mean only that it obeys laws, and obeys the same laws under the same circumstances. If tables had a habit of walking away or of exploding without giving

[1] Montaigne, drawing generously on classical pyrrhonists, made a great slaughter in *Raymond Sebond* of those who pretend that human senses can yield any reliable information. The answer to him was given implicitly but triumphantly by the band of inquirers who were even then creating modern science.

notice, or if the sun appeared in the morning only when a free, irresponsible, undetermined and indeterminable gremlin willed it to appear, science would vanish also in spite of the stability of the human sensorium.

In art the situation is different. Art consists in stable objects —the texts, for instance—but it impinges on certain human faculties which are only in part fixed. These are of course the emotions and the whole complex of taste and moral value. Fortunately, human instability in regard to emotion and value runs a limited gamut. The human repertory is finite, and in some respects even narrow. The result is that the artist can hope to communicate at least with a segment of mankind, and that the critic can establish "valid" rules or criteria. But both are threatened at all times with obsolescence; for example the artist who believes that the sacrifice of prisoners endears the conqueror to us, or the critic who asserts that the troubles of the lower classes are subjects fit only for comedy, is eventually left behind. He thought, no doubt, that he had appealed to a stable, perhaps to an eternal human value; and he lost the game. Another, who relied on the "permanent" appeal of a farewell between a soldier and his wife or his child, guessed right—so far in history, at any rate. We must steer carefully, in other words, between the view that criticism is impossible because "everything is a matter of taste," and an imprudent confidence that criticism can become a science. Voltaire thought that Shakespeare's heroes were barbarians. We often accuse Corneille's of being rhetorical machines. The quarrel between the English and the French approach to tragedy illustrates the instability of the human receptor. On the other hand, Voltaire knew that Hamlet was a good man and that Claudius was a villain; and we recognize in Corneille's *Le Cid* that Chimène is a heroine. Instability, then, but within limits.

We repeat that criticism will endeavor to call on the most widely diffused and most reliable values and emotions in order to attain a measure of validity, except in cases where its avowed intention is to formulate an ephemeral judgment. The same ideal holds in the work of classification and definition. In eliminating effect, whether emotional or intellectual, from the definition of tragedy, our purpose was precisely to avoid the contingent and the unpredictable elements which, had they been admitted, would have given us a map with fluctuating borders. To say that Iago deceives Othello is to make a valid, "stable" statement. We are fairly safe from the currents of history, climate, geography, and personal temperament. To assert that Shylock commands our sympathy is more dangerous; we are already on precarious grounds; we cannot arrive at a unanimous opinion. To affirm that *Oedipus* leaves us with a feeling of triumph is to thrust into darkness, as experience shows. And what is so dubious with respect to a single work becomes chaos when an entire genre is at issue.

Our question now is whether the definition of tragedy which we have advanced does in fact give us the stability and security of a scientific proposition; or, if not, whether it relies on emotions and values stable enough to make at least for a general and a lasting concurrence. In the following restatement of the definition, the questionable sections are italicized.

A work of art is tragic if it substantiates the following situation: A protagonist *who commands our earnest good will* is impelled in a given world by a purpose, or undertakes an action, *of a certain seriousness and magnitude;* and by that very purpose or action, subject to that same given world, necessarily and inevitably meets with *grave* spiritual or physical *suffering*.

Whether "grave suffering" will occasion much controversy may be doubted, and it is perhaps unnecessary to defend it. The criterion for what is, and what is not, intense pain for a protagonist seems to have varied little or not at all through the ages. The problem does not arise at all, needless to say, if the protagonist *asserts* that he does, or does not, suffer. It might arise only in the simple exhibition of a situation: sickness, separation, exile, death. But in practice our notion of what situations conduce to unhappiness is so stable that we may proceed in the assurance that "grave suffering" refers to a stable human pattern.

"Earnest good will," however, presents real difficulties. It will be noticed that we have used the psychological term rather than the moral term "goodness." "Good" must have an umbilical

cord running to a mother system, and our concern is to detach
the work of art from any preordained ethic or metaphysic.
Good will is a psychological event which precedes all ethical
patterns, whether in the history of the species or in the development of a single individual, and which outlasts any specific system. Nevertheless, we will use the word "good" in our discussion
with the understanding that it is given its purely popular, un-
doctrinaire meaning.

That goodness in the protagonist is an absolute requisite of
tragedy is beyond question. For ultimately tragedy depicts an
evil in life, and the fall of the unsympathetic, of the evil, is the
opposite of evil. While tragedy does not demand a specific emotion such as distress or sadness as an after-event, it does appeal
to our (stable) sense of value in requiring that we recognize
together unfortunate events, and that we accept them as unfortunate, even though we may not be actively moved.

This brings us to an important point. Tragedy concerns a
hero on whom we are to bestow our good will; but it need not
concern a hero who really *excites* our sympathy. We perform an
intellectual act, in other words. Chimène is in the category of
acceptable heroines, even if she leaves us actually rather indifferent. The fact of tragedy does not depend on petty or local likes
and dislikes. In actuality the situation is the same. We do not
befriend all those with whom we sympathize "in the abstract,"
and often we judge that evil has occurred, that a good man has
fallen, without undergoing an answerable emotional experience.

This is why bad tragedy is a possibility. It is the tragedy in
which the fate of a sympathetic protagonist leaves us indifferent.
In Philippe Quinault's tragedy *Astrate* (1664), we can all recognize (if we are brave enough to read to the end) that Elise,
who kills herself in order that her lover may be true to his duty
(which consists in killing her), is a sympathetic figure; I mean,
one who conforms to our standards of virtue or amiability. That
the situation is fantastic, and that the play is worth no more
than its printer's ink—that we remain unmoved—does not alter
the fact. Bad as well as good tragedy requires an event which is
evil; and it is evil when it happens to someone who receives
even our coolest approbation.

But beyond this, it cannot be denied that perfect agreement in approbation, whether active or tacit, can never be obtained. Historically, a certain shift has taken place from the noble to the agreeable hero, from the "admiration" which Minturno added to the Aristotelian pity and fear, to the fellow-feeling which made the bourgeois and then the proletarian protagonist a reality. But this shift is not important, for it did not materially alter the references of good will. Even some of the classicists recognized that social status was only a *"parure étrangère,"* an alien adornment, not of the essence. [2] The history of Western art has seen no revolution in appreciation and sympathy. We do not share the medieval hatred of the Jew or the ostensible Renaissance abhorrence of the atheist, and the louse-infested hermit saint may have departed from our category of the good; but these are ripples rather than tides.

Of much greater consequence are the differences which occur in any given age among those who directly converse with each other. In the current quarrel of the moderns and the ancients, [3] the question is whether there are twentieth-century heroes. We have seen that those who, like Mr. Krutch, demand that the hero have some cosmic importance, engage with us in a previous dispute concerning the meaning of tragedy. Others, however, who require no more than our own good will, merely feel incapable of extending it to naturalistic figures. The problem goes back as far as to Balzac. Does Eugénie Grandet have enough stature to command our good will? It acquires a great interest in the case of *Madame Bovary*. Do we or do we not like Emma well enough to turn the work, which in every other respect is perfectly tragic, into a genuine tragedy? Is *Germinal* a tragedy? Is Hialmar in *The Wild Duck* sufficient for a tragic figure? Is Kafka's K. a sympathetic protagonist? Can a modern American writer rise from the muck long enough to create a personage in whom we feel even a theoretical interest?

It is obvious that our demand for "good will" rather than "stature," "heroism" or "true nobility" is so minimal—we are concerned, after all, with the *least* common denominator for

2 Fontenelle, sec. 7.
3 See section 9.

tragedy—that we are making ample room for modern tragedy. Contemporary tragedy is as natural a development from bourgeois tragedy as the latter was from heroic tragedy. The ancient spectacle of inevitable overthrow is still the matter of today, in *The Old Man and the Sea* and in *La Peste* and in a hundred other places; and good will is not killed even by behavioristic psychology. But we must make our peace with the element of instability which does enter into our definition, and *any* definition. It does not allow for automatic and universal application; it is not the perfect map. Whether Richard III or Emma Bovary or Kutz commands our good will cannot be decided "objectively." Even a knowledge of the author's intention does not help, for the author may mean to write tragedy without succeeding. It is *our* good will which must be elicited. All we can affirm is that the area of instability here is altogether insignificant compared to the area of common consent. Tragedy demands that an evil have occurred; no man can be compelled to accept the common view of what is regrettable; presumably therefore Mr. Hyde's list of tragedies (if he granted our definition) would differ somewhat from Dr. Jekyll's; but by and large men do feel in common, and even a gangster may be found sobbing his heart out over an orphan in a sentimental film.

Our good will, we say, must be earnest. By the same token the tragic action must have seriousness. Since the reaction will depend largely on the action, we must consider these two points together. Once more we must grant a no-man's-land, or rather an any-man's-land, in which a real uncertainty will exist as to certain works. Do children or animals make suitable tragic heroes? That is to say, are they capable of serious treatment? Treatment is, of course, of the essence here. It is quite possible for an author to seize upon a situation which is potentially grave, and to turn it into a fantasy or a lyric entertainment. The result will seldom be controversial. Oscar Wilde's tale *The Nightingale and the Rose* illustrates our point. It shows the tragic mechanism, and it employs a theme which, in other guises, is one of the staples of tragedy; yet *most* people will not receive it as a tragedy because it does not seem to demand an earnest response. A Student looks for a Red Rose so that his love will dance with him. But to his great sorrow he cannot find his Rose. The Nightingale hears his lament; she thinks he is the perfect lover, and determines to find the Red Rose for him. The Student's own rose tree eventually tells the Nightingale that she must press herself against a thorn and sing all night long in order to obtain such a Rose. The Nightingale agrees, and lets the thorn stab her all night, singing, "Death is a great price to pay for a red rose, and Life very dear to all. It is pleasant to sit in the green wood, and to watch the Sun in his chariot of gold, and the Moon in her chariot of pearl. . . . Yet Love is better than Life, and what is the heart of a bird compared to the heart of a man?" She dies in the morning, and the Student perceives the Red Rose on its branch; but as it happens his love rejects him for the Chamberlain's Nephew, and so the Student goes back to Metaphysics.

Other illustrations of character and action potentially serious yet modified by a peculiar treatment can be found in many libretti. Quinault's *Armide*, written for Lully, will serve as a ready model. *Armide* is like a masque, full of spirits, magic, songs, set in the land of shepherds and shepherdesses. Armide has reduced Renaud, whom she both loves and hates, into a coddled inaction by certain magical operations. Renaud abandons glory for love; but in the end, Ubalde's magical shield undeceives him—he tears off his garlands and furbelows, and casts off his Armide. But going back to glory means abandoning love, and he does abandon it with great regret.

This uses once more the outer mechanism of tragedy, but seems too slight to engage us seriously. We are not thinking, it goes without saying, of the seriousness of the personages themselves in such works. Even in comedy and in farce, the characters themselves can be perfectly serious. Earnestness is the result of a compact between the artist and ourselves over the handling of any action and character whatsoever. The compact is usually successful; but we must allow for the possibility of disagreement. Does *Measure for Measure* engage us in earnest? Does Dr. Stockman in *An Enemy of the People* earn our serious good will, and is his action handled with gravity? Neither of these would be tragic even if we answered in the affirmative, but they would come very close to tragedy. They can be cited, at any rate, as doubtful cases of seriousness, as grounds for dispute.

We conclude again that these portions of our definition rely on a stable, but less than perfectly stable, system of emotions and values of mankind; or at least in Western man. Our map is not, and can never be, final, but it satisfies almost all our requirements.

And the conclusion is unaltered by the last question, that of magnitude. Corneille, in the *Discours de l'utilité et des parties du poème dramatique*, speaks for the whole world when he asserts that tragedy *"veut pour son sujet une action illustre, extraordinaire, sérieuse."* [4] Illustrious, that is to say, having magnitude; extraordinary, because the very possession of what we call tragic purpose sets the hero apart from the mass of the population; and serious, as we have already seen. Tragedy, we know from the outset, is a "strong" word, like catastrophe or disaster. The only question is whether the idea of magnitude commands a response stable enough to be useful. Is there such a thing as a tragic short story? Possibly some persons will affirm that magnitude involves a certain length, a degree of formal spaciousness. Our own feeling is that magnitude is not irrevocably tied to length; that importance (which is the same thing as magnitude) can be expressed in the briefest compass. *The Lady of Shalott*, for example, has enough magnitude to qualify as a tragic narrative. Lawrence's *The Rocking-Horse Winner*, brief as it is, exhibits not one but two simultaneous tragedies, of the mother and of her son. And, for all their concision, the Gospel narratives dealing with the betrayals of Peter and Judas appear to be full tragedies of guilt. But this is not a subject on which legislation is possible. We rely on actual stability; our confidence is empirical, not prescriptive.

Chekhov's short story *Vanka* puts the whole question in the most forceful way, for whether tragic or not it is a small masterpiece. A little country boy, sent to the city by his indigent grandfather, writes a letter in which he complains in the most pathetic terms that the master to whom he is apprenticed beats

4 "Tragedy demands for its subject an illustrious, extraordinary and serious action." Corneille, I, 25.

and starves him. He begs his grandfather to come and take him away. Having finished the letter, full of hope, he addresses it "To Grandfather in the Village," steals out of doors to mail it as someone has told him to do, and returns to fall asleep amidst sweet visions of deliverance. Here the story stops.

Is the boy too small to be tragic? Is this merely "pathetic"? Here is a situation whose external form at least is that of the incompletely shown tragedy.[5] The little hero, by sending his letter away, performs an action which is to him of the greatest importance. His hope is foredoomed, however; the action bears the seed of the actor's disappointment. But whether the action, as well as the character, has sufficient magnitude may well be a matter for contention.

The story, incidentally, points up the connection between magnitude in the action and magnitude in the character, as well as that which exists between magnitude and earnestness. Yet these are not all equivalent concepts. Many a narrative falls short, or falls short for certain members of the public, because the action of a sufficiently important protagonist is not in itself great enough to qualify as tragic. Small causes may have grave consequences, as Pascal points out, speaking of the grain in Cromwell's urethra which changed the course of the world. Agamemnon, in Aeschylus' play, meets his death simply by returning home. Creon, the King of Corinth in *Medea*, dooms his daughter by granting Medea one day of grace before her banishment, for the respite gives her time to proceed to her vengeance. The Duchess of Malfi babbles a little, and thereby fatally reveals to the evil Bosola that Antonio is her husband. The lack of magnitude in these actions is, it seems to us, obvious. Vanka's, on the other hand, is subject to doubt. That of Oedipus, beyond quarrel.

In short, whereas the demand for pity and fear or for any "vision" surrenders the concept of tragedy to a *Through-the-Looking-Glass* world (" 'What's the use of their having names,' the Gnat said, 'if they won't answer to them?' "), the requirements of earnestness, good will, and magnitude leave us with a useful concept, one with a world of recognizable and generally

5 See section 13 for this species of tragedy.

accepted referends. We need a concept which is not only intelligible (for the effect-definitions do not want intelligibility), but also transitive—that is to say, pointing to distinct objects. Were tragedy a quality, like beauty or pathos, we would not define it in terms of sensible objects; but tragedy is not a quality; it is a situation.

Part Two

13 · Tragedy in Relation to the Whole Work

THE TRAGIC situation is not necessarily the whole work of art as we find it, say, in *Oedipus* or *Madame Bovary*. Though it fulfills all the requirements of the definition, it may occur as only one section of a larger piece. The tragedy of *Heracles*, for instance, has its real beginning in the middle of the play: the first half of the play concerns itself with Heracles' deliverance of his family from the usurper Lycus. Corneille, in *Rodogune*, quickly sketches in a tragic dilemma, when Rodogune requires of her lover that he kill his mother; but this is only one episode in a long intrigue. Sophocles' *Ajax* opens with a tragic madness, but swiftly turns to the hero's death and the question of his burial. In *Bajazet*, the hero, who is almost all the time a victim depending on Roxane, becomes a tragic hero for one moment, when Roxane, in the fifth act, gives him a choice: either he must marry her and kill his beloved Atalide, or refuse to marry her and die.[1]

In the midst of the endless ramblings of Schiller's *Don Carlos*, one tragic incident occurs. The perfect Marquis Posa sacrifices his life in order to allow Carlos to escape to Flanders and accomplish a great liberal mission there. But this is only a moment in the two-hundred-page play. The tragic story of Dido is but one episode in the *Aeneid*. In the *Idylls of the King*, the tragic guilt of Lancelot and Guinevere does not coincide with the whole poem.

1 This shows, incidentally, that a character may *become* a tragic hero during the course of an action.

99

Again, in Hardy's *Woodlanders* the most striking episode is possibly tragic, but it forms only one link in the life of Grace Melbury. Giles Winterbourne, strong man of the woods, pure to a fault, but ill as it happens, protects the unhappy Grace, who is flying from her faithless husband. Giles gives her his own house, and from his excessive delicacy refuses to enter it. He takes up quarters in an exposed shed. It rains, the storm blows, and Giles grows more and more sick; still, he refuses to enter the house, and bravely meets death rather than offer the slightest offence to his love. [2]

A final example is Malraux's *Condition Humaine*, in which we find two brief tragedies: the terrorist Ch'en's self-immolation in his attempted assassination of the villain Chiang Kaishek; and the choice offered by Police Chief König to Kyo, between betraying the cause by working for him, and being tortured to death.

If many tragedies are preceded by much non-tragic activity, many others continue beyond the downfall of the tragic protagonist. The detailed discussion of post-tragic episodes must be left for an appropriate section. But it may be mentioned here that this last portion of a work can be artistically very important. In it may take place the redemption (over half of *Lord Jim* is concerned with this), or some other form of restoration. *Crime and Punishment, The Mill on the Floss, Alcestis, The Scarlet Letter,* Ibsen's *Little Eyolf* would not be complete if they ended at the moment when the tragedy closes. Other works, on the contrary, embitter the calamity through the post-tragic action. In the Goncourt brothers' *Germinie Lacerteux,* the servant girl is pursued beyond the grave by her mistress' disappointment in her; while the wicked daughters in Turgenev's *A Lear of the Steppes* thrive after their father's death.

Further, it may happen that an author does not show the whole tragic action at all. He may present a section of it, and imply the rest, or he may even let the whole tragedy have occurred before the beginning of the work. This happens in Aeschylus' *Persians:* Xerxes is the tragic hero; he has tried to

2 The question here is whether we can offer Giles our *earnest* good will.

cross "the sacred Hellespont" in his war against the Greeks—

> swelled with thoughts
> Presumptuous, deem'd, vain mortal! that his power
> Should rise above the gods' and Neptune's might.

For his pride, he has been inevitably punished by a complete defeat. But all this has taken place before the play, and now the ghost of Darius reports the facts to Atossa, Xerxes' mother. The play, therefore, is a lament after a tragedy.

Riders to the Sea is quite similar in this respect. Here, too, the sons of Maurya dared affront the power of darkness itself, the unconquerable sea, and perished one after the other as a result. To be sure, the last son's foolhardy attempt is portrayed, but this is the last spasm of a long sequence. The play is rather a mother's lament—"the end of all the songs man sings."

In the case of T. S. Eliot's *The Cocktail Party*, on the other hand, the principal tragedy—that of Celia Coplestone's sacrificial death in "Kinkanja"—occurs during the action of the play, and yet it is made known only by report. Celia's initial tragic decision—the decision to seek God—does take place on stage; but the decision made, Celia disappears from view.

Sometimes we enter when the tragic purpose has already been adopted. We have before us the tragic action full-blown. This is the case with Sophocles' Ajax, whom we meet directly in the midst of the rage which will cause him an unbearable shame—unless indeed we think that his real tragic action was the original defiance of the goddess, occurring before the play, for which she avenged herself by inflicting madness on him. *Alcestis*, too, shows us the sacrifice of the heroine in full career, as it were. Alfieri's *Mirra* opens with the girl in the throes of her incestuous passion. The same applies to Phèdre in Racine's play.

Sometimes, we see only the overthrow, as in *Ghosts*, in *Little Eyolf*, and (as far as Hester is concerned) in *The Scarlet Letter*. Again, the author may lead us up to the performance of the tragic action, and let us guess at the overthrow. We think of Prometheus' final defiance, which leaves him exposed to the tortures of Zeus, and *Portrait of a Lady*, which closes as Isabel decides to return to her husband.

The point is that tragedy is a concept; it is not a particular form, like drama; it is not a form requiring a special kind of diction (Aristotle recommends, if he does not require, a mixture of the common and the unusual); it is not the conveyor of a specific emotion or a specific world-view; it serves no specified imposed function in reality (whether purgation, improvement of our morals, expansion of our power to sympathize, or allaying of mental conflicts); it handles or taboos no specific subject matter; and, finally, it obeys no specific structural plan. Tragedy occurs when the tragic situation is represented in art briefly or at length, whether or not it is represented with a beginning, middle, and end; whether or not it has unity of time, place, and action; whether or not its action is likely, probable, or impossible; whether or not it has a scene of recognition, a climax, or even a staged reversal.

14 · Hero and Victim

THOUGH WE CAN consider hero and purpose separately, the most striking characteristic of the tragic hero as a personality is just his possession of a purpose—a drive or an ideal which insists on being gratified. The tragic hero rises above the common ruck by the very fact of his purpose, even when it is a guilty one. He has stature, in other words; he has climbed, and therefore he can fall. "The inactive," says Seneca, "reach hoary age, and in a lowly state but secure stands the mean lot of a humble home; from a lofty height ambitious courage falls." And, in a sense, all tragedy concerns ambition; more fundamentally, all tragedy concerns the will.

That is why we eliminate from our category the serious work of art which concerns itself with a victim; not because such a work must be inferior—by no means—nor because it evokes a particular kind of emotion impossible to confuse with the tragic emotion; but simply on conceptual grounds. Tragedy deals with an *action* harmful or fatal in its nature. The fatality which reaches us "out of the blue" is one thing; that which we call upon ourselves by our will and our deed is quite another; and the distinction is so decisive that—to recur to the opening sections of this essay—the same term cannot properly be applied to them.

Yet though the difference is radical, some critics continue to confuse the two genres. To cite but a single example, one of the most competent of the English writers on tragedy, F. L. Lucas, extols Turgenev's *A Month in the Country* as the very flower of modern tragedy. In fact, however, the heroine, Viera, is completely at the mercy of the older Natalia, her protectress and rival in love, who snatches (though not successfully in the end) Aleksiei away from her. Vera's sudden growth from girl to woman is touching, perhaps, but it has nothing to do with tragedy.

Many works deal entirely or principally with victims. They repeat in one way or another the theme expressed by Gloucester in King Lear:

> As flies to wanton boys are we to the gods;
> They kill us for their sport.

This theme of uncontrollable fatality is probably older, because more elementary, than that of tragedy. It is illustrated by a whole period, the medieval, in which it was thought to be the very essence of tragedy.[1] And it has recurred as a theme typical of the West in its old age, when men seem to have lost the power to act in a straightforward and determined manner, and have become flies to a variety of modern boys. *The Cherry Orchard* is a beautiful instance of this weary species of drama.[2]

Perhaps the most literal dramatizations of Gloucester's maxim occur in Hardy's novels; and the most famous of his perfect victims is Tess, who is seduced as a young girl and abandoned by her one-day husband when she tells him this fact.[3] From that point on, the doomsters buffet her from misery to more misery, until she ends her days swinging on the gallows. Jude the Obscure is no luckier: that lugubrious manikin, or Schopenhauerian imp, little Father Time, decides to slaughter himself and Jude's children with him; whereupon Sue loses her faith and becomes a Christian, returns to her former husband, and leaves Jude to die a victim of alien forces he understands but cannot master. Hardy's philosophy (if we can flatter him with this term) makes tragedy all but impossible.

---

1 At least one modern critic, J. S. Smart, explicitly accepts the medieval concept of the Wheel of Fortune—"the conception of undeserved, unexpected, and crushing calamity"—as truly tragic (p. 10).

2 But Chekhov's greatest play, *The Three Sisters*, is a perfect "continuous" tragedy (see section 18).

3 Telling her husband is of course an action, and to that extent Tess is unimpeachably tragic.

We have already seen that "realistic" tragedy exists. Nevertheless, it is true that pure naturalism, as practiced by Zola and his successors (especially in America), is hostile to the tragic concept; not, however, because it rejects heroic values, but because, in it indictment of society, it naturally tends to deal with victims. The wanton gods are no longer creatures living in the clouds, but social forces; yet the effect is the same. Evil social forces either make purpose impossible—the human being is flotsam—or they make men so ugly that they cannot, however we pity them, evoke our good will. Either purpose or good will gone, we are left with something other than tragedy. Thus Edmond de Goncourt, in *La Fille Elisa*, portrays a girl whom a cruel environment destines to a brothel from her very birth. Faulkner's idiot, in *The Sound and the Fury*, or his Christmas, in *Light in August*, are stunted before they can begin life on their own. We pity them, we cry out against the world, but they do not obtain our good will. Gervaise in *L'Assommoir* does nothing: circumstances turn her from a good woman into an animal, and finally kill her. Similarly, in George Moore's *Esther Waters*, the heroine is helpless; she must allow the winds to blow her wherever they see fit; by pure chance, in this case, they finally blow her to a snug haven. It is the same with Maupassant's *Une Vie*, which may partly have inspired Moore's novel.

And yet, Zola himself was not incapable of creating tragic figures. In *Germinal*, for example, the protagonist, Etienne Lantier, is inspired by a grave and "noble" revolutionary ideal; while, on a somewhat lower level, the wretched working woman, La Maheude, seized with a sudden enthusiasm, obtains a foredoomed yet heroic vision of world justice. A real naturalistic tragedy is Daudet's *Sapho*. In this novel the hero, Jean Gaussin, becomes (as the phrase goes) the slave of his passion for a common woman. He hates a love which smothers and besmirches him, and yet for a long time he cannot shake himself free of it. The tragedy is redoubled after he has succeeded finally in breaking with his mistress: he goes back to the world, begins a career, and engages himself to a pure young girl. But then the call comes again: like Antony, he must return to his

bewitcher—the tragic drive is love, the inevitable accompani-
ment is shame, horror, and the loss of worldly hopes.[4] On the
periphery of naturalism, finally, we come upon Emma Bovary,
who is possessed by an ideal not untainted, but one which lifts
her far above the vegetating bourgeoisie. Her dream of ideal
love, vulgar as it is, contrasts powerfully with the satisfied im-
mobility of her husband and with Homais' longing for the
Croix d'Honneur.[5]

If the works of the naturalists abound in victims, many great
or merely famous plays and novels of the past have shown them
the way. Aeschylus' Agamemnon, for instance, simply falls a
prey to Clytemnestra. In Euripides' *Phoenissae*, which concerns
the same battle for Thebes recounted in Aeschylus' play, the
emphasis is all on the victims: Jocasta, Creon, Antigone, Oedipus; while the flight of the two brothers before Thebes seems to
be little more than the occasion for the comments and laments
of the inactive participants. Webster, in his most famous work,
portrays the Duchess as purely a victim. In Rowe's *The Tragedy
of Jane Shore* Jane is also a hapless toy in other people's hands.
And more recently, Grillparzer's *Die Jüdin von Toledo* provides
an interesting example. The flighty but attractive Rahel entices
the King of Castille—and thus far she is an active protagonist.
But after she settles down to be the king's mistress, she becomes
the helpless butt of the court's intrigues, and is finally murdered
in the king's castle. Thus a tragic hero can "degenerate" into a
victim when two actions, logically unrelated to each other,
occur.

There is no requirement that a tragic hero must suffer more
than a victim. Deianeira, in Sophocles' *Trachiniae*, inadvert-
ently poisons her husband: she can swiftly expiate her error by
a suicide; but Heracles, the victim, is left in the throes of a
long physical agony. The same is true for Meleager in Swin-

4 Daudet adds somewhat gratuitously to the irony when Gaussin loses
even his Cleopatra in the end. This final depressing touch is, however,
"accidental" and not an intrinsic part of the tragedy. For the question
whether a man who *acts* as a *victim* of an overwhelming passion can be a
tragic protagonist, see the next two sections.

5 In section 6, we raised the question whether the novel is tragic, but
did not answer it.

burne's play. Degree of suffering, in short, is not a criterion by
which we can distinguish between tragic and non-tragic personages.

Victims, then, however much they move us, are not and cannot be tragic figures. The fate of Othello differs radically from
that of Desdemona. But the disparity lies in the objective situation, not in the emotions that they engender. For both may
evoke pity and fear, and admiration, and awe; both may be
equally pathetic. But Othello is undone by his own will;
Desdemona by Othello's.

If tragedy is a situation, then the often-heard opposition between "tragic" and "pathetic" must be invalid. For we cannot
contrast a situation with an emotion. When we say of a character that "he is not tragic, but merely pathetic," it is because we
have implicitly defined tragedy by a *severe emotion*. But in fact
nothing prevents a tragedy from being pathetic; we may shed
feminine tears (if we are so inclined) for Goethe's Werther
without therefore cutting him off from his status of tragic hero.
And, in the end, who will say that Oedipus is *not* pathetic as he
stands revealed to himself, or as he cries farewell to his children?

Returning to the tragic hero, we may note that he is not
necessarily a single person. A protagonist can be a group or even
a whole nation,[6] even when the author imposes on the mass
some leader who gives the narrative a focus. Frequently, too, a
work contains two or more distinct tragic figures.[7] A good case
in point is *Antigone*. For even if we disagree with Hegel's view
that Antigone and Creon are equally right, we still have to admit
the latter as a fully tragic character. He is a grand though sinful
figure, comparable in stature to Macbeth. Indeed, it is not impossible to read the play as particularly concerned with him
rather than with Antigone. It opens with Creon's sinful decree,
and develops with his stubbornness in enforcing it. As a result

6 Well-known examples, not all of them tragedies, are Hauptmann's
The Weavers, Zola's *Germinal*, Gorki's *The Lower Depths*, Malraux's
Man's Hope, O'Neill's *The Iceman Cometh*, and *Galsworthy's Strife*. The
greatest work in this category is, however, Cervantes' *La Numancia*.

7 Examples are *Le Cid*, *Andromaque*, *Phèdre*, *Paradise Lost*, *Faust*,
Billy Budd, and *Beyond the Horizon*.

of this stubbornness, Antigone gives up her life, and brings about in turn the death of Haemon and Eurydice. She vanishes well before the end of the play, leaving Creon, whose tragic purpose has involved the destruction of his whole family, alone in the shambles.

The tragic hero does not have to be the center of interest in a work of art. This is a corollary to the assertion that a work may not be tragic in its entirety, and may simply include a tragic episode. In the *Phoenissae*, as we have seen, the tragic heroes play subordinate roles. So does Gregers, the tragic figure in *The Wild Duck*. It is to be supposed that if we speak of "a tragedy," we *usually* mean that its central action is tragic. But since tragedy is a situation (or an idea about life), we must expect to find it occasionally as a side issue in a work of art concerned with something else.

Our last question concerning the tragic hero is whether he must have a flaw. This question may take two forms, though we can usually ignore the distinction. Under the first form, the contention is that the hero falls *because* of the flaw in his character. In our terms, this is to say that the tragic purpose is not wholly spotless; that all tragedies are to some extent tragedies of guilt. Under the second form, it is asserted simply that the hero who falls must not be a pre-eminently virtuous man. In other words, the particular purpose which unavoidably dooms him may be laudable, yet the man as a whole has his faults. The first form is the doctrine of the *hamartia*. As everyone knows, the meaning of that term is to this day a matter of high dispute. It is not known whether Aristotle meant by it a moral weakness, an intellectual blindness, or even, as has been suggested recently, a mere mistake in identity.[8] What matters to us is that centuries of criticism assumed that he did mean moral weakness, and, furthermore, that he was right in demanding it. But even if he did not demand that the protagonist fall because of his imperfection, he did beyond question forbid the fall of a perfect hero.[9]

8 Else, pp. 379 ff.
9 See 1452b. I will use the word "perfect" very loosely. A perfect hero in literature is simply, for our purpose, a figure presented with full approbation.

Whichever form the proposition takes, it appears to be the by-product of some basically optimistic orthodoxy. Such an orthodoxy would affirm, in one language or another, that the wages of sin is death, and the wages of purity long and prosperous life.[10] If, according to this view, a man falls, we may be sure that in some way he deserved it, for God or the Cosmos would not allow his destruction otherwise. A more sophisticated optimism might admit a discrepancy between the error or flaw and the *degree* of suffering, but this still insists on a measure of dessert—on justice, in short. The most sophisticated optimist, finally, can argue that the perfect hero may *seem* to fall, and indeed does suffer in the flesh, but that his virtue is his triumph: in that sense, the pure hero cannot fall even if he wants to.

Cultivated men might not contend that this kind of justice was what life obviously offered, but—is art supposed to reproduce precisely what life offers? It might be the function of art to idealize, or to warn, or to instruct, or to improve; "to range," in Sidney's words, "into the divine consideration of what may be, and should be"; [11] and then it would be an act of subversion on the part of the artist to depict a moral order in which it is normal for a paragon to be destroyed. Normal: for to the simplest audience as to the best-trained critic, the work of art is irrepressibly symbolic; it always seems to expand the assertion it makes concerning one man to an assertion concerning mankind. Hence the danger of pessimistic art in the eyes of the high priest and the governor; hence their demand for at least

10 This simple affirmation appears in one of the choruses of *Agamemnon*:

> Sin, not prosperity, engenders grief;
> For impious acts breed their own kind,
> And evil's nature is to multiply.
> The house whose ways are just in word and deed
> Still as the years go by
> Sees lasting wealth and noble sons succeed.
> (*Vellacott's translation*)

Such a view appears also in the Hebrew chronicles and in the simple medieval *exempla*. We may suppose, indeed, that when the pious chronicler has to record a defeat for his hero or his people, he will if necessary invent a sin for them in order to leave God clean.

11 Sidney, p. 10. Hesied tells us that the Muses "to all ills/oblivion yield, to every troubled thought/rest," or, as we should say, that the function of art is to provide escape. (*Theogony*, tr. Else, 11, 78–80.)

an approximate poetic justice (with justice, of course, defined in the terms they choose), even if the poem or the film touches but on the single life of a poor unaffiliated Jack.

One wonders whether Aristotle's doctrine of the not pre-eminently virtuous hero does not hang more than it should on his ethical theories, and not enough—for once—on pure observation of the plays he had before him. He admits, of course, the effect of chance in upsetting a man and bringing even the virtuous to grief, and he has no love for "happy endings." But the *Ethics* unequivocally insists that the real source of happiness lies in a man's own mind, and that happiness consists in the habitual pursuit of virtue. The perfect man—the man without *hamartia*—is he who intelligently practices virtue. This pre-Stoic doctrine makes light of external "accessories" to happiness. We can easily supply the bridge between the *Ethics* and the *Poetics*. If the universe (which is itself a harmony, an order, a good) is so constituted that the good man is happy in his virtue, it must be shocking, odious, and in fact unreal to depict the utter despair of a pre-eminently virtuous man. This is not a demand for poetic justice, of course, for it allows the moderately good man to suffer more than he deserves, and the perfect man to be deprived of by no means negligible external goods. But the man whose reason is his king cannot be touched by despair. At best, he emerges from his suffering even nobler and therefore, in a deep sense, happier. At worst, he cannot be utterly destroyed. If Oedipus had been a pre-eminently virtuous man, the spectacle of his prostration would have been an immoral one.

It is generally recognized that Greek practice did not conform to Aristotle's requirements. With respect to the perfect hero, we need think only of Hippolytus, the perfect youth whose flaw could only be the Christlike one of being too pure; of Prometheus; or of Antigone. And Oedipus? Here we must distinguish between the two forms of the argument which we have just exhibited. If we interpret Aristotle merely as requiring that the hero, whatever the cause of his fall, be imperfect, then Oedipus fits the case. Sophocles has gone out of his way

to give Oedipus a choleric complexion. But if the *hamartia* is a
moral flaw and if this moral flaw must be the direct cause of the
hero's destruction, Aristotle and Sophocles part company. Oedipus' pugnacity has no bearing on the tragic action as such,
namely his inquiry—for the inquiry is the tragic purpose—and
the fatal disclosure. His quarrels with Teiresias and Creon do
not affect the outcome; the second quarrel is, in fact, a curious
intrusion, one of those "episodes" which Aristotle condemns,
for it serves no purpose in the structure of the plot. All this is
in sharp contrast with the rashness of Coriolanus, which does
occasion the latter's downfall. We do not need to dwell on this
point. Oedipus conforms, at any rate, to the chief requirement
of the moralist, that the man who falls have a fault to show for
it.

We remain with the fact that the Greek dramatists were
willing on occasion to portray the undoing of flawless heroes, if
need be to the scandal of the moralist. This is the rule, however
moot one or the other example of it may be. What of Christian
tragedy? Here we find an important class of faultless tragic
protagonists, namely those who renounce the world, even to the
point of death. Antiquity has Antigone and Iphigenia to show
(no one sacrifices himself in Homer, however), but the genus
flourished only under Christianity. In Christian tragedy the
spotless hero gives up property, safety, health, domestic affection, and life itself for the glory of God. He may do this as
cheerfully as Socrates drank his cup, in which case there is no
tragedy. But Christianity does not demand this extreme. The
hero may suffer bitterly in the flesh and in the soul as a result
of his renunciation. His saintliness may entail a daily struggle
and a daily wretchedness. If the good in him conquers, it does
so, like Antigone's, exacting as its price all earthly happiness.
True, such tragedies are invariably followed by the gathering-up
of the soul into paradise, but these are post-tragic redemptions; [12] the tragedies themselves still stand. Suffering, as Ivan
points out in *Karamazov*, is irredeemable. Incidentally, what is
true of genuine Christian tragedy is true also of the pseudo-

12 See section 21.

tragedies of Fortune. The medieval artist was free to demonstrate that in this sublunar world the Wheel might swing down for even the purest man.

Tragedies of renunciation, in which the hero chooses the better but grieves in giving up the worse, are perfectly compatible with orthodox morality. Medieval tragedy portrayed the *suffering* of perfect heroes, but not, it must be admitted, their spiritual undoing. It made no room for the subversive tragedy in which the City of God itself proves a mirage. In other words, in the tragedies concerning perfect heroes which are written under such an orthodoxy, we encounter always an element of victory. Aristotle seems to be safeguarded by the Middle Ages better than by his own models. The saint, says medieval tragedy, may suffer, but he cannot fall. And Shakespeare "obeys" Aristotle even more literally. Aside from Romeo, who is a truly medieval victim—a happy man destroyed by a wrong turn of the Wheel of Fortune—Shakespeare's major protagonists are all less-than-perfect figures. More than that: they fall *because* of their flaw. If Aristotle did chance to mean that this was tragedy, he would have had good cause to applaud. Brutus, Macbeth, Othello, Lear, Antony are all men who were perfect once (still in our loose sense of the term), but who were corrupted along the way, acted out their corruption, and *therefore* fell.[13] Hamlet's case is more doubtful, because the play itself is so dishevelled, but is he not corrupted too from perfect resolution to sinful indecision?

The case of French classical tragedy is more obscure and entertaining. At first sight, it seems as though it flies brazenly in the face of Aristotle's rule. *Le héros ne doit jamais avoir tort, et il faut lui en épargner jusqu'à la moindre apparence. S'il a un mauvais côté, c'est au poète à le cacher, et à peindre son visage de profil.*[14] *Only* perfect heroes will do, say the French; and, indeed, the so-called tragedies of the great age make a

13 This does not, I hope, involve us in the Bradleyan notion of justice after all. In Shakespeare's world, the best men are weak: the devil corrupts whom he pleases, and nothing seems so hopeless as virtue.

14 The hero is never to be at fault, and he must be kept free of the least appearance of wrong. If he has a bad side, it is up to the poet to hide it and to paint his face in profile. Fontenelle, sec. 42.

grandiose exhibition of paladins Greek, Roman and Oriental. But the poets extricate themselves by means of the happy ending. Does Aristotle command that the perfect hero shall not fall? Then we will save him, just when all hope seemed impossible. This is the *tragédie heureuse* of that happy age. It merely forgot the further precept of Aristotle, that tragedy ought to have an unhappy end! Only Racine, though he never admitted it, managed to inflict serious and *final* suffering on flawless heroes; namely on Hippolyte and on Titus.

We have seen that in the past the most common species of tragedy which admitted the suffering of flawless protagonists was the still "moral" one whose hero gained a spiritual victory even as he groaned. Only a few works are bold enough to arraign the universe by demonstrating that the virtuous purpose of a virtuous man can by its own nature, inevitably, lead to the man's annihilation. Even today we are offered fine examples of the elevating kind of tragedy: Arthur Miller's *The Crucible* is one. But many modern writers, abandoning at last all allegiance to a trumpery piety concerning the moral beauty of the world, frankly depict the spectacle, already offered in *Hippolytus*, of innocence destroyed by itself, and obtaining no solace and no salvation in exchange. This is the world of *Billy Budd*, for example—though Melville does not have the toughness to let his hero die conscious of the futility of angelic virtue—of *The Castle*, of *The Plague*, of *Waiting for Godot*. Far from demeaning all the heroes of old, as some critics have charged, modern literature often exonerates man at the expense of the universe. Under the "absurd" regime, the search for happiness of innocent men does not lead to a spiritual victory in spite of suffering or death, but to death "without hope or consolation."

This is not, as we have seen, an utterly new kind of tragedy. But as we search the past for instances, it is a surprise to find one—hinted at least—where we would least expect it, namely in the story of the death of Christ. If we consider this story with perfect naïveté, rid of all religious or theological preconceptions, we may find in it a touching early example of the downfall of a perfectly innocent tragic hero, whose tragic purpose—let us name it vaguely—is to bring in his person the Word of God among men. This purpose—the struggle of a lone man against the world—leads him inevitably to his death. But is not this death a foreseen, foredesired, happy event? Here is where our story becomes so remarkable. For Jesus does not die, like Socrates, at peace and content. He suffers. Luke and John, to be sure, carefully expunge the tragic despair of Jesus as it is ingenuously reported by Matthew and Mark. With them, Jesus is beyond tragedy, a fellow to Socrates. This makes Matthew's account all the more interesting. Here Jesus appears little different from other prophets of the time who died as a result of dangerous experiments involving their kinship with God—of *hybris*, in short. Jesus, we know, had boasted that he could raise up the Temple in three days (John, 2:19 and Matthew, 26:61); now, near death, he assures his disciples that he could cause "more than twelve legions of angels" to appear for his rescue (Matthew, 26:53); to Caiaphas, a little later, he says that he will be seen "sitting on the right hand of power, and coming in the clouds of heaven" (26:64). But these are his public utterances. In private, he prays three times that the cup may be taken away from him (John omits this painful circumstance), though he is willing to submit: "Nevertheless not as I will, but as Thou wilt" (26:39). Already he is a tragic figure. He does not die gladly. But the real *coup de théâtre* occurs at the end. The Jews taunt him: "He trusted in God; let Him deliver him now" (27:43). Even the thieves join in. Jesus does not answer. But his last words are like an admission. He cries, "My God, my God, why hast thou forsaken me?" Let us note that he does not ask *whether* God has forsaken him; but *why*. The terrifying implication is that God *has* forsaken him. The tragedy is consummated, and Jesus perishes like his fellow prophet who thought that God would open the Red Sea for him and who drowned instead. He has an Oedipean recognition, the classical *anagnorisis*: he had fancied himself the Son of God, but God, he sees, has abandoned him.

Luke's account is significantly different. Here the last words of Jesus are, "Father, into Thy hands I commend my spirit" (23:46). John is noncommittal, and, incidentally, most down-to-earth. Jesus recommends a disciple he loves to his mother; he says that he is thirsty; and his last words are, "It is finished" (19:30). Only in Matthew and in Mark is the full tragic misery of Jesus given, with an appealing disregard for the theological difficulties raised by his despair. How different this is from the busy, zealous and gleeful self-immolation of later martyrs, for whom death is the sheerest release! Even without the final *Eloi, Eloi, lama sabachthani*—"My God, my God, why hast Thou forsaken me?"—Christ has submitted with a heavy heart to the personal catastrophe which was the inevitable consequence of his mission; even then he is tragic. But the last scene gives an almost "naturalistic" sense of cosmic futility.[15]

It will be objected that I am ignoring the resurrection. This, it is true, refutes Jesus' own pessimism, and proves that God had not forsaken him after all. Once more, however, we are dealing here with a post-tragic episode. It colors our feelings, of course; we are not allowed to despond for long. But the tragedy has nevertheless been accomplished. Musical versions of the Credo illustrate the point. The gloomy *Crucifixus*, ending in *"et sepultus est,"* is corrected, but not abolished, by the outcry of *"Et resurrexit"* which follows at once.

Another objection might be that after all Jesus is only quoting the first verse of Psalm 22—it is not his own cry of despair. But an examination of Psalm 22 makes his particular choice even more remarkable. The first twenty-one verses reproduce his own despondency and indeed his concrete situation. But from verse 22 to the end the psalm—somewhat inconsequently—turns to the praise of God. Why does Jesus choose the first verse? "My God, my God, why hast thou forsaken me? why art thou so far from helping me, and from the words of my roaring?" (our recollection of the full verse makes his cry even more poignant in its allusiveness). He might as easily have chosen verse 24: "For he hath not despised nor abhorred the affliction of the

15 Jesus' cry of despair has caused a great deal of bafflement among theologians. The Exegesis and Exposition in the recent *Interpreter's Bible* (vol. VIII) express an honest irresolution. Usually, the answer has been sought in the double nature of Christ. That of the early heretic Cerinthus, reported by Gibbon, is as good as any: the Christ as eternal power (*aeon*) and Son of God, forsook the mere man Jesus at the Passion, and left him to suffer and to complain as a mortal being.

afflicted; neither hath he hid his face from him; but when he cried unto him, he heard."

In sum, we dismiss the doctrine of the imperfect hero or the tragic flaw as irrelevant in the definition of tragedy. Not only is tragedy no justification of the universe by definition, but even when it does portray the heartrending fall of a spotless hero, no obligation can be laid on it that the fall be balanced by a spiritual victory in another quarter of experience by which universal good is safeguarded.

15 · The Question of Free Will · 1

THE TRAGIC protagonist must be "impelled by a purpose."

What is the source of that purpose? The definition is silent on this subject, and speaks neither of free will nor of necessity. We refer, of course, to free will or necessity in the *tragic* purpose, not in any other action which may occur in the work. Is the protagonist tragic only if he freely chooses his goal? Does he cease to be tragic if an Apollo or an Iago manipulates him; if a passion overwhelms him; if he acts in a dream or in a fit of madness; if the gods have predestined him; if he is ignorant of what he does; if he acts against his will?

The issue of free will does not seem to have been raised in discussions of tragedy before the German romanticists began to advertise it. With them, however, it became fashionable to think of tragedy as a freely willed action struggling against an external necessity—that is to say, some hard decree laid down by the gods, or anything inexorable. Not all critics demanded this freedom. Schelling, curiously, *required* that the guilty action should be enforced upon the actor. Necessity induces the crime, which the hero later freely expiates: *"Dass das überlegte und freie Verbrechen gestraft wird, ist nicht tragisch,"* he asserts flatly.[1] But most critics felt, and many still feel, that if the actor does not freely will his deed (whether it be a crime or a virtuous action), "he is mean, contemptible, and nothing worth." [2] He becomes what they call a puppet—their favorite

1 "The punishment of premeditated and free crime is not tragic." Schelling, p. 347.

2 O'Neill, Jr., p. xxvii.

117

analogy. "We are the playthings of the gods. . . . We . . . remain in the hands of the Great Sculptor," [3] and this is to many an intolerable situation which demeans man and renders tragedy impossible.

It is possible—and even tempting—to dismiss the entire question as a pseudo-problem, a verbal hocus-pocus without experiential content. Free will is a term more easily used than understood, while the difference between logical and psychological freedom has as yet to gain enough currency to make communication on this point easy. If we take up the issue at all, it is only because the history of modern criticism forces it on us by its own insistence. Even so, instead of submitting a reasoned defense of determinism in tragedy, we will limit ourselves to an inquiry into the practice of the Greek poets, even though questions of free will and determinism do not appear to have been posed in Periclean Athens. If the Greeks made "puppets" of some of their heroes, we will assume that the question is settled, for we have premised all along that their major plays cannot be shaken off as referends for the word "tragedy."

Now it is simple to demonstrate that Greek tragedy often disowns free will in its practice, and that it trusts to the tragic power of necessity. Of necessity there are, however, several kinds, which contemptuous references to "puppets" blend together and obscure. In the first and crudest, the actor is manipulated *with or against his will* by an immediate external force. This would seem to reduce him to a puppet indeed. However, unlike the puppet, he can suffer and, strange to say, even feel a horror of himself as a result of the action which someone or something forced him to take.

The second kind of necessity is fatalism as to the conclusion. Somewhere, in the book of the gods, it is written that the actor must *eventually* perform a certain deed—such a deed that its very nature will be fatal to him. But this seems to leave open at least the possibility of some free will. The gods have said that the hero must arrive in Rome; but he might go there by way of Moscow or by way of Madrid; he might arrive tomorrow

3 Dixon, p. 93.

or in a year: the gods do not say. There is a grim Chinese story
which illustrates the point. Once there was a man who sat in a
spacious golden room. At one end of the room he could see a
dark and narrow passage, but he did not know where it led. A
spirit appeared and said: "You may remain here if you desire,
or if you wish you may go through the passage." The spirit
vanished. The man hesitated a long time, but finally decided to
walk into the corridor. This corridor led him to another room,
as spacious and golden as the first. And again the spirit appeared, and gave him a choice like the first; and again the man
decided to go through a dark passage, and arrived once more in
another room. This was repeated a certain number of times.
Sometimes the man decided to remain in a room for a while,
sometimes he went on at once. At last, he encountered a tall
man with an axe in the middle of a passage, and the man cut
off his head. But this did not really make any difference; for,
the story tells us, the executioner would have cut off his head
in any case, whether he had stayed in a room or not.

The third type is complete fatalism. The gods have pre-
scribed not only the end, but each step toward that end. This
does not mean that they despatch a Hermes to prod and push
the actor at each point (as they do in the first species). Usually
the events will seem to happen "naturally"—the unfortunate
hero may never suspect that a certain event did not occur by
"chance," but was all the time plotted and predestined.[4]

The fourth kind is an internal necessity which we call motivation, passion, or simply character. Schelling, speaking of
Shakespeare, writes: "*An die Stelle des alten Schicksals tritt bei
ihm der Charakter, aber er legt in diesen ein so mächtiges
Fatum, dass er nicht mehr für Freiheit gerechnet werden kinn,
sondern als unüberwindliche Notwendigkeit desteht.*"[5] Under
this category, when we ask why the hero performed a certain
action, the author replies (through the text), "because he was

4 At the fringe of tragedy, this species of determination occurs frequently in prophetic passages: *viz.*, Cassandra's vision of what is to come in
Agamemnon or Prometheus' prediction of Io's career of suffering.

5 Schelling, p. 368. "In lieu of the old Fate he has personality, but he
gives the latter so powerful a compulsion, that it can no longer be counted
as freedom, but rather appears as insurmountable necessity."

this or that kind of a man, because he had such or such a motive." Then, however, we may feel that the motive does not explain everything, and that there is still an element of spontaneity between motive and action. Or else we may be satisfied that the action has really been accounted for. Much depends on how detailed a psychological explanation the author provides. But if we continue, and require to know *whence the motive*, we must beware of leaving the vicinity of tragedy, and fetch necessity or free will at five or six removes. Tragedy gives us a fatal action: our question applies exclusively to its motive, or at most the motive behind that—not to a source of the action lost in the past, long before the first word of the text, but to the values directly relevant to the action.

It is clear that these four kinds of necessity should not be mistaken for each other: that the fourth kind, for example, is very far from simple fatalism. Can we really assert that directly a man is deprived of free will he becomes a puppet? To be sure, if a man's action is determined in advance by a god, he is in some sense the god's toy, although the term obliterates the suffering, the shame, the horror which the so-called puppet may feel. But if a man's action is determined by an uncontrollable motive, then, if he is a puppet, that puppet seems to pull its own strings, which makes it a strange puppet indeed!

We touch here on the delicate subject, not so much of freedom as of "our consciousness of freedom," a consciousness which is often taken as incontrovertible proof of the existence of the thing itself, though as evidence it reminds one rather of Dr. Johnson's cavalier refutation of Berkeley. The consciousness of freedom is regarded as proof that man is not "a mere object." But does determinism reduce man to a mere object to begin with? Does man become an item tossed about by "forces"? By no means. Such "forces" impel him through the colossally intricate mediation of his nervous system; in other words, they manifest themselves as his very own motives and desires. This is what we mean when we say that the puppet seems to pull its own strings. The wind blows, the tree bends: that is inanimate nature. But if the blowing wind makes the tree *want* to bend before it bends, then the tree will acquire a "consciousness of freedom." We experience the absence of freedom only when our desires are thwarted—usually from the outside. Conversely, the experience of freedom is no more than that of being impelled not by wind, king, or witch, but by one's own desires. To be the "puppet" of one's own desire—with desire itself the "puppet" of one's total psychic history—that is free will. That is why we see men and women, whose motives seem to us so clearly mere functions of their life histories, assert, with a vehemence only we ourselves match in like circumstance, that they *chose* to do thus or so.

Properly speaking, then, we would argue that the fourth kind of necessity which we have exhibited here is what actually goes in the world by the name of free will, especially when two desires—left and right arm of the puppet—clash, and the individual hesitates. However, we waive the point, accept for the sake of argument the distinction between internal necessity and free will, and insist instead that the distinction among the four species of necessity which we have listed ought to be kept in mind by the careful critic. "Without this indestructible feature of a man's will [i.e., freedom]," goes a typical statement, "there could be for art no tragedy at all. The absolute quiescence of fatalism kills all dramatic significance of character." [6] Such a statement disregards three vital facts: first, that fatalism is not quiescent; second, that absence of free will, and fatalism, are two very different things; and third, as we shall see, that all forms of necessity, including fatalism, are compatible with tragedy.

IT IS A CRITICAL COMMONPLACE to see in the *Oresteia* the depiction of a world passing from one moral or legal order to another. The old order is that of the Furies, themselves older than Zeus: it is the order of the primitive vendetta in which blood simply calls for blood, an eye for an eye, a tooth for a tooth, and the individual will counts for nothing. A man is asked what he did, not why he did it. The new dispensation—that of the younger gods headed by Zeus—calls presumably for our kind of justice,

6 Courtney, p. 43.

which involves a weighing of motives and an examining of circumstances and intentions, as well as the admixture of mercy to the pitiless legalism which had existed before. Since in Orestes we have at last, in Mr. Kitto's words, "an avenger who is not following evil desires of his own," he can be forgiven under the new law.

The latter half of this interpretation, though many repeat it, wholly lacks textual support. It is, in short, an imposition of our own culture on that of Aeschylus, and amounts to little less than bowdlerization. Orestes is not exonerated in the final judgment on the basis of character—to wit, his selflessness; nor because he had a moment's hesitation before killing his mother (that, if anything, was a weakness); nor, certainly, for feeling remorse, for he is not touched by it. On what ground, then, is he acquitted? The first and simplest answer is that he was ordered to kill by Apollo, who, it is underlined time and again, is the voice of Zeus. At this level, we are dealing merely with a change of command. Zeus supersedes the Furies. We do not yet inquire in what Zeus consists; we know, so far, that whatever his nature, whatever his law, his nature and law are to take precedence over the Furies'. But we can go one step further at once, and see that Zeus is the god of the *polis:* his law will at any rate be administered by a public court of justice (as demonstrated in the *Eumenides*), and thus supersede the private, or family, law of the vendetta. Another immediately visible consequence of the new order is that the law of the Curse is wiped off. In the future the law—Zeus' law—is to decide guilt or innocence. Another Agamemnon will be avenged through a judge in the city, not by his son. And he will not be avenged automatically, as the vendetta demands, but only if the court finds against the assassin. The accused man will be arraigned, tried according to a definite method by an institutional body, and, whether he is acquitted or condemned, his case will end at the moment of verdict. Such is the new, the Athenian law.[7]

Already Orestes can be set free, since he acted as the agent

7 The Furies are the carriers of the curse which starts the interminable chain of the vendetta. They are obvious "divinizations" of a social pressure for private vengeance which, as we know from many modern survivals, becomes an obsession for the injured relatives. Where the *polis* does not

of the new headquarters, which is accountable to nobody.[8] But this is too crude, and the question remains whether Zeus' order of assassination, as transmitted by Apollo, was *wicked*. For the new dispensation is concerned to justify itself, and even to integrate the old order into its own as far as possible. The justification is given in plain words by Apollo and Athena. It is so silly by modern standards that civilized critics, who are not inclined to see much levity in Aeschylus elsewhere, argue that here he has his tongue in cheek, or that, at any rate, he cannot possibly have meant what he said. This is drama, says Mr. Kitto, not argument. But if Aeschylus is serious anywhere, surely he is serious at this most solemn moment of a very grave play, a moment in which the divine and the patriotic are revealed as one. Orestes' crime, it appears, is a much smaller one than that of Clytemnestra, for the death of a woman is a lesser thing than that of a man (and a king into the bargain), and furthermore the mother is not really kin, as is the father. However unpleasant this sounds to our ears, such is the text; Aeschylus is serious; and with this we remain.

We now have two reasons for Orestes' acquittal, neither of which has anything to do with Zeus the merciful god, or with the purity of Orestes' intentions.[9] There has been no inquiry

---

exist, or is ineffective, and men must take justice into their own hands, the kinfolk are under such terrifying compulsion, internal and social, that they may well invoke the presence of Furies. The gods symbolize this pressure, but they are also convenient higher sanctions for a human drive which brooks no gainsaying. Orestes himself describes in vivid terms what happens to the man who would free himself from the demand of the vendetta: fangs, ulcers, pus and the like will plague him (*Choeph.* 11. 278 ff). An early example of the law of the vendetta occurs in the *Theogony*. The series of intra-family revenges from Uranus to Cronus to Zeus is said to "make amends to the vengeful spirit of Father Sky." The best modern treatment of the theme of vendetta morality versus civil law is undoubtedly Mérimée's *Colomba*.

8 Athena: "From Zeus was offered testimony clear, and he that himself uttered the oracle himself bare witness that Orestes should not suffer harm for his deed." *Eum.* 11. 797–99 (here and in the following pages I use the Smyth translation of the *Oresteia* in the Loeb Classics).

9 So bedevilled are commentators by this matter of the pure heart and free will that we are not surprised by the blankest contradictions within, if need be, a single sentence: e.g., "Orestes commits his terrible deed of vengeance voluntarily, and for pure motives, at the express command of a god." (Greene, p. 107.)

into Orestes' motives, nor any indication that Zeus acts out of mercy. If we ask why Clytemnestra, who also stood incontrovertibly under a higher legislation when she murdered Agamemnon, cannot be exonerated, the chief answer must be that she had the misfortune of carrying out orders from cashiered generals, i.e., from the system of *Moira*, the principle of the Curse, the whole *family* system of the vendetta to which the Erinyes belong, and which Zeus of the *city* has dismissed. The only other reason given is, as we have seen, that her crime is a graver one than that of Orestes. Nothing is said concerning her darker, perhaps more selfish, motives. Selfishness, in fact, is not a vice for the Greeks.

But now we can take a final step and define in what Zeus' new dispensation consists. The reason given for Athena's ballot —that the death of Clytemnestra was less weighty than that of Agamemnon—turns out to be of small importance, serious though it is. What matters is just that a reason is given at all. Not mercy; not psychological extenuation; but Persuasion is the new motif:

> I am grateful to Suasion [says Athena after the verdict] that her glance kept ever watch o'er my tongue and lips when I encountered their fierce refusal. But Zeus, *he that sways men's tongues*, hath triumphed.[10]

That is to say, the automatic principle of the Curse, which demands blood for blood as mechanically and unthinkingly as earth attracts a stone, is now replaced by the rhetorical debate (a popular pastime in Greece) of which Aeschylus immediately supplies an example; in brief, by Reason, by Thought. *Dike* makes way for *Nous*. Zeus' law is the law of Reason. Clytemnestra's relatives, represented by the Furies, no longer have the right to pursue Orestes as a matter of course; they must present a case and argue—for example, whether a mother is or is not to

10 *Eum.*, 11. 970–73. (Italics mine.) "Their" refers to the Furies. Here is Vellacott's translation: "Holy Persuasion too I bless,/who softly strove with harsh denial,/till Zeus the Pleader came to trial/and crowned Persuasion with success." (Penguin Classics, p. 179.) Lattimore has "I admire the eyes/of Persuasion, who guided the speech of my mouth/toward these, when they were reluctant and wild./Zeus, who guides men's speech in councils, was too/strong." (Chicago, 1953, p. 169.)

be regarded as blood kin. In this instance, they happen to lose the debate. Apollo, after directing the sacrifice of Clytemnestra, wins the case for his client on reasonable grounds—reasonable to the Greeks and not to us, perhaps, but reasonable nonetheless. That debate will later begin to delve into motivation we know from many sources, Euripides' plays foremost among them. But that is not the main point at any time, and it is not a point at all in the *Oresteia*. The finale of the trilogy, comparable to the final chorus of an oratorio, does not speak of mercy, nor of free will, nor of pure motivation; it extols Persuasion, Law, and the glory of Athens.[11]

What is the place of free will in this process? Even if all that we have said so far is discounted, the fact remains that the tragic event in the trilogy, namely the murder of Clytemnestra, exhibits as clearly as possible our first species of necessity, a direct manipulation by a god:

And I [says Orestes] when I came back home—an exile I had been beforetime—I slew her that gave me birth—disavow it I will not—in vengeance to requite the murder of my sire I most dearly loved. And for this deed Loxias, in common with me, is answerable, who, to spur my purpose, threatened me with cruel woes should I fail to do this deed upon the guilty.[12]

Already in *Agamemnon* Cassandra has asserted that the revenge of Orestes is predetermined:

Yet we shall not perish unavenged of Heaven; for there shall come in turn another, our avenger, a scion of the race, to slay his mother and exact requital for his sire. . . . For a mighty oath hath been sworn of the gods that his slain father's outstretched corpse shall bring him home.[13]

What is Orestes but a puppet of the gods? Surely the conten-

11 It is also noteworthy that a king—for Orestes is now king—submits to the Areopagus. Tyranny too is displaced by the Law. As Gilbert Murray points out in his *Aeschylus*, our man was a republican, conservative though he may have been.

12 *Eum.*, ll. 462 ff. When Orestes says "in common with me"—the phrase is variously translated but with the same effect—he means that Apollo found in him a willing tool; but still a tool, as is shown by the fact that Orestes quickly yields the floor to Apollo, who is in turn a tool of the Olympian "boss."

13 *Agam.*, ll. 1278 ff.

tion that he is free to choose between obedience and disobedi-
ence of Apollo is absurd. The most that can be said, as we have
already indicated, is that he acted as a willing and remorseless
instrument of heaven.[14]

Aeschylus, we conclude, made a tragedy in which external
manipulation negates man's will. For Orestes is tragic beyond a
doubt. He acts, he has our good will, and he suffers as an inevitable condition of the action itself; and this is tragedy.
Clytemnestra, we may add incidentally, seems at first freer than
Orestes, but it is made quite plain that she too is the instrument of fate. She illustrates necessity as to the end but not as
to the means: though she must kill Agamemnon, she might
have killed him under different circumstances. Aeschylus seems
to be aware of the fact that she could easily become sympathetic, and so turn into a tragic person too; in the *Choephori*,
therefore, he goes out of his way to blacken her with incidental
actions—for example, her mistreatment of Electra. Had Aeschylus allowed her a little more virtue, we would have had on our
hands two tragedies of fated guilt.

We have observed that, even though it is Apollo who com-
pels him, Orestes can still be considered guilty under either
dispensation, at least to some extent. For half the votes are cast
against him in the end, the Furies are admitted into the new
order, and such retribution as they have already exacted from
Orestes is not repudiated. How, we may ask at this point, can a
man be compelled by God, predestined even from before birth,
or even crazed when he acts, and still be thought guilty? The
question is raised rather commonly by Greek texts. To resolve
it, we must keep in mind the inconsequence of motivation in
the old order, in the eyes of the Erinyes. Where we speak of
sin, the Greek will refer to pollution. Pollution can be defined
in modern terms as the state of guilt without the condition of
sin. Its characteristic emotion is horror rather than remorse. A
man may kill his father by some mischance: even today he will
feel a horror akin to that experienced by the polluted "crimi-

14 When he hesitates a moment before the murder, Pylades reminds
him of the oracle. "Count all men thy enemies rather than the gods."
(*Choeph*. 1. 902.)

nals" of Greek story. Thus, even though Orestes claims many
times that his deed was a just retribution, he still exclaims,
after the murder, "My victory is a pollution none need envy." [15]
One can, in short, do a just deed and yet be polluted—and this
is of course the very tragedy of Orestes' act.

It is convenient to cite here similar cases from Euripides'
Orestes and *Electra*. In both plays, the actors and the gods
themselves continually reiterate Orestes' fundamental innocence (in the Christian sense): Apollo is explicitly blamed for
the command he gave Orestes—"Drag him [Apollo, that is]
then to your bar, put him to death." And yet, at one point,
asked by Menelaus what consumes him, Orestes replies: "Conscience: the conscious guilt of horrid deeds." This would be a
meaningless inconsistency if we did not translate guilt as horror. Orestes, then, in Euripides as well as in Aeschylus, is forced
into a crime, and is therefore polluted rather than guilty.

We have seen in the *Oresteia* a remarkable case of necessity
by direct manipulation. Sometimes, however, only the end-
point of an action is foredoomed. This may be the case with
Oedipus' curse upon his two sons, as we hear it reported in
Seven Against Thebes. They are to kill each other, but it is not
established that they must come to this pass at the moment
Eteocles "chooses" to oppose his brother. To be sure, if he goes,
he must die, and this is what makes his going tragic; but did he
have to go? Here free will may be invoked, if the reader wishes.
But it is not a very useful free will: for, like our Chinese hero,
sooner or later Eteocles must have his head chopped off.

The situation in which an end is definitely established, but
the means left free—or at least subject to the hero's own
motivations—can present some prickly artistic problems. On
one occasion, it must have cost Sophocles a deal of head
scratching. We know the plot of *Philoctetes*. Neoptolemus, as
Ulysses' lieutenant, must carry off the bow and arrows in
Philoctetes' possession, for without them Troy cannot be taken.
Neoptolemus finds the wretched, ill, and embittered Philoctetes
on the island of Lemnos, where Ulysses and the Atreides for-
merly abandoned him. He obtains the weapons by deceit, but

15 *Cheoph.*, 1. 1017.

remorse overcomes him, and he subsequently returns them to Philoctetes, who refuses to repair peaceably to Troy with the Greeks. Neoptolemus is about to carry out his (tragic) decision, give in to Philoctetes and leave the Greeks to their fate, when Heracles appears, bidding Philoctetes return to the siege with the weapons.

Why did Sophocles have to invite a *deus ex machina* in this and not in the other extant plays? The most plausible answer is that, on the one hand, he wished to show the tragic hesitations of his hero, Neoptolemus, and the latter's final *free* decision against social and political obligations, in favor of justice and righteousness (the same issue as that of *Antigone*); but on the other hand, he was dealing with a case in which the end had certainly been set by the gods: *of course* Philoctetes was to return, and Troy to be won. The dilemma between justice and social duty had become here a struggle between free will in the process and predestination in the end. And Sophocles settled the matter by proving, in effect, how useless free will really is when the head must come off anyhow. Neoptolemus made his free choice to obey Philoctetes, and Philoctetes stuck to his perhaps free decision to stay away from Troy; but a moment later Heracles, worried no doubt that his two sheep might be straying too far from where the gods wanted them, predestined them back to the fold. Sophocles had gained both points, that of righteousness and that of historical truth, but at the price of an artistic failure.

Is Oedipus a tragic figure? He is more, he is the very none-such of tragedy. And yet, as one critic puts it, "throughout he has been a puppet in the hands of Fate; so far as purpose and even consciousness are concerned, it is not he but Fate that is the agent." [16] We cannot discover, nor is it important that we know, which of the two kinds of fatalism we encounter here: whether Oedipus had his freedom when he slew the voyager at the three highways, or whether (as is more likely) the gods negotiated this extraordinary meeting, and filled Oedipus' breast with rage, and put the sword in his hand. At any rate, in ful-fillment of the curse on the Labdacidae, Oedipus must sin *even-*

16 Vaughan, p. 44.

tually and feel all the horror of his pollution. Again, his decision to institute a search for Laius' killer, and then for his own
identity, cannot be viewed as a free one, but only as the final
act of the gods in bringing home the *effect* of a crime that had
never bothered him. We may read in *Oedipus at Colonus* the
philosophical commentary on the action. Again and again,
Oedipus affirms his innocence, in contrast with the real and
free sins of Creon, Eteocles and Polyneices. "Was I the sinner?/Repaying wrong for wrong—that was no sin,/even were
it wittingly done, as it was not./I did not know the way I went."
And he arraigns the gods: "*They* knew;/they, who devised this
trap for me, they knew." [17] And later, speaking of the "murder
and incest/and all the events that have thrust themselves upon
me," he once more asserts that "the gods so willed it—doubtless
an ancient grudge/against our house. *My* life was innocent.
. . ." [18] As a man more sinned against than sinning, Oedipus
grows in this late play to a sublime stature: the great Sufferer
led into crime by the mysterious gods, then purified and later
sanctified by sorrows; and it is the peculiar beauty of the action
here that we need no Athena, as in *The Eumenides*, to inter-
vene and cast a ballot in order to break the curse. The years
themselves, and sorrows nobly endured, have washed King Oedipus clean of his stain; his pollution, that is, rather than his sin.

An interesting example of predestination as to the end, but
not as to the way to the end, occurs in the *Iliad*. Achilles is undoubtedly free to choose between a long and tranquil but in-
glorious life at home, and a short but magnificent life in battle.
But after he has made his choice, it is not known how and
when he will be killed. All he has—and this it is which gives the
epic its elegiac grandeur—is the knowledge that some time soon
he is fated to die. Nevertheless, Achilles is genuinely free, since
he does have a choice between life and death; whereas Eteocles
and Polyneices do not have any choice at all..Aeneas, on the
other hand, is directly manipulated by the gods; he is the puppet
of all puppets, and yet his separation from Dido is tragic too,
since it tears his soul. It must be confessed, however, that if the

17 E. F. Watling's translation (Penguin Classics), p. 86.
18 *Ibid.*, p. 110.

Aeneid does not breathe with the vigor and haleness of the
Iliad, this is due in part at least to that constricting control of
the gods.

But to return to the drama. In Euripides we face at once
something more modern and something more chaotic. His plays
are earthier than his predecessors', less reverent, and less unified.
He does not seem to set great store by philosophic or theological
consistency; sometimes his incompatibilities are glaring. Yet at
the risk of some oversimplification, we may assert that whenever he takes the blame away from Fate or the gods, and leaves
his characters floundering in their mere humanity, he endows
them with full responsibility for their actions. This means, in'
Christian terms, free will. But on the other hand, he does not
rid all his plays of the older forms of necessity. The upshot is a
philosophical eclecticism which does no damage, however, to
the individual pieces.

Now that character is more "human," and now that the protagonists are to be held responsible for their actions, we are not
surprised to find long speeches and regular debates concerning
blame or innocence, along with an inquiry into motives which,
as we have seen, hardly interested Aeschylus. In *Andromache*
Hermione complains to Orestes that the "evil women who came
to her and puffed her up" caused her to plot against the life of
Andromache. Iphigenia in Tauris admits no blemish on the
gods for the sacrifice of her person in Aulis: the blame, according to her, rests entirely on the Greeks. Hecuba, in *The Trojan
Women*, similarly ridicules Helen's defense, in which the latter
had appealed to the guilt of the three goddesses, and insists that
Helen freely willed to run off with Paris. Typically, with the
new human way, we read real character studies, such as those
of Medea and Admetus. Here and elsewhere, Euripides shows
himself an adept psychologist; but never to the extent of lifting
responsibility from these actors. Agamemnon, in *Iphigenia in
Aulis*, is a good example. Hearing the oracle, he decides to yield
his daughter as sacrifice; but even while she is coming, he has
changed his mind, and appears before us as a devoted father.
Thereupon Odysseus and Calchas threaten to rouse the armies
against Agamemnon and Menelaus, and to have Argos destroyed

if Iphigenia is not handed over to them. They leave Agamemnon in a desperate quandary. Here is no Fate which has decided beforehand whether Iphigenia will be sacrificed or not: we are made to feel that the destiny of Greece really depends on the free decisions of Agamemnon and Iphigenia herself. We say "free," for though there is enough motivation here to satisfy the determinist that Agamemnon is caught between two equal valences, and as little a free agent as Gervaise in *L'Assommoir*, Euripides plainly believes in the capacity of man—and therefore his obligation—to act not according to motives, but according to his vision of the right. Thus Iphigenia herself, who gradually foregoes her personal inclinations and hatred of death, and at last decides "to give safety to Greece, and conquest to her arms" by offering her life, plainly makes an ethical choice. This is unquestionably meant to be a free choice: "Freely now I sink in night."

Clytemnestra in *Electra* also deserves to be mentioned as a psychological study. It is a notable and characteristic fact that Euripides has set aside the theme of the curse on the house. As a result, unlike Aeschylus' Clytemnestra, who pleads that "Fate bore a share in these things," Euripides' queen utters an elaborate defense of her actions in terms of domestic motives.

In a number of important cases, Euripides, following every author's right to mince or prolong explanations as he pleases, simply presents a crucial action without any explanation at all, or with only the barest appeal to some standard of morality or conduct which has been, presumably, freely adopted. The best known example is that of Hippolytus, who is presented very simply, and very beautifully, as a youth devoted to chastity. Even a novelist well read in psychology might have the taste to introduce a person without a genetic account of his character. Hippolytus is under no curse, no doom; presumably, he has freely chosen to be chaste.

Similarly, the two tragic figures of *The Bacchae*, Pentheus and his mother Agave, are represented as having freely condemned and banished Dionysus. We may also mention two self-sacrifices besides Iphigenia's, that of Menoeceus in *Phoenissae* and the more famous one of Alcestis.

But Euripides is far from maintaining his pre-Christian morality consistently. As often as not, he exhibits the crudest form of tragic necessity, i.e., actual command and manipulation by a god, the nontragic equivalents of which are the orders of the *dei ex machina* who descend on so many of his plays. In *Hippolytus* itself, Phaedra's tragic passion is lit by Aphrodite against Phaedra's own will as a part of her revenge on Hippolytus. She also manipulates Theseus' error and curse on his son: "Men may well commit an error when gods put it in their way," says Artemis in the final reconciliation.

But the most extreme instance of manipulation is afforded by *Heracles*. For no reason at all except Hera's standing enmity, Iris and Madness appear: "Hera is minded to brand him with the guilt of shedding kindred blood by slaying his own children," says Iris. We are back in a primitive world order, and in this case there is not even an ancestral sin to expiate. At any rate, this is the very opposite of free will. Heracles is maddened, and in this mad state he butchers his wife and three children. Notice that he is not a mere victim, like Oswald in *Ghosts:* he *does* something which carries in itself and involves by its very nature his own suffering. Nor is he quiescent, for when he wakes, instead of sitting down as a puppet should, he raves in utter despair. Like Oedipus, like Orestes, he is not guilty in our sense, but "confounded," "polluted," to use his own words. This, by the way, is made even clearer in Seneca's *Hercules Furens*. Amphitryon proclaims the hero guiltless. "What man anywhere hath laid on error the name of guilt?" But Hercules replies, "Oft hath great error held the place of guilt." He has a "tainted spirit"; but, of course, he has not freely committed a sin.

Madness is not an ideal form of tragic purpose, but its fitness cannot be questioned. Only on the surface does Heracles have less control over his destiny than Oedipus, Aeschylus' Orestes, or Euripides' own Phaedra. Actually, these tragic actions are one and all directly manipulated by the gods. And so is the madness of Sophocles' Ajax and Euripides' Agave, though both of these are involved in a larger tragedy—namely, a sane but guilty defiance of the gods.

As a last example of direct manipulation, we should mention

Euripides' Orestes, as he appears in *Electra* and *Orestes*. Even though Euripides has removed the theme of the curse, he has left, and even emphasized, the command of Apollo. Indeed, the two plays flatly arraign the god, and accuse him of being the cause of Orestes' sufferings. Nonetheless, Orestes is a tragic hero: the assassination of his mother entails, in advance, some form of dire punishment.

Euripides offers at least one instance of a predestined end without predestined means. In *Ion*, we have an extremely complicated intrigue, in which we feel that matters might go differently at any moment. Yet the end is laid down: Ion must be accepted by Xuthus as his son, and by Creusa as hers.

Several times, too, we are given a picture of total predestination: Aphrodite in *Hippolytus* plans out her whole campaign, during which two actors—Phaedra and Theseus—must be made to commit tragic actions. Again, Cassandra in *The Trojan Women* foretells to Agamemnon the fatal shock that awaits him; and Castor and Pollux sketch out in *Electra* the days to come of Orestes; but the predestination of the last two examples is not of tragic events.

Enough has been done to show that in the Greek drama absolute freedom existed side by side with the most severe necessity. As no cause can be shown why, in aesthetic objects, the opposition between free will and necessity is so important that one of them should be thrown out of court; why, in other words, Iphigenia should be and Oedipus should not be a tragic figure; we will be wise to accept the observation of an anonymous translator of Schiller a century and a half ago: "It is a singular phenomenon, that the . . . principle of Fatalism, while it urges on to the perpetration of the most flagitious acts, has in reality no effect in weakening the moral feeling, or in diminishing that remorse which is attendant on the commission of crimes. . . . On the contrary, there is something in our nature which leads us the more to compassionate the instrument of those crimes, that we see him consider himself as bound to guilt by fetters, which he has the constant wish, but not the strength, to break." [19]

19 Schiller, *The Robbers*, London, 1800, p. xiv.

16 · The Question of Free Will · II

FATALISM and the curse have vanished, by and large. The examples of it in Western literature are usually deplorable, as we discover in Schiller and in many a pretentious romantic drama, for the Fates cannot easily be transplanted into modern Europe.[1] Calderón, in *La Vida Es Sueño*, gives the theme of predestination a Christian topicality, and does so very well. But most authors have exchanged the predetermined end for Schelling's *Fatum* within the character. In a sense, the god has simply been transferred from Olympus or Sinai to a position inside the man. No longer does an Apollo appear, pointing the way. The pointing god is *within*; and if Orestes was the puppet in Apollo's hands, now we think of him as the puppet of his own motives.

But both spontaneity and necessity are compatible with tragedy. In by far the majority of cases, authors neither tell us outright nor give us enough information to assure us on this question; and whatever they do, nine times out of ten, they can be claimed by both parties. If they supply abundant motivation, the determinist will be satisfied, but his opponent will insist that between motive and action there is a chink of freedom which the animal vision of the necessitarian fails to register. On the other hand, many authors—even mechanists—do not wish to be bothered with psychological inquiries. Therefore they

1 Herder defines tragedy as the struggle of man with Fate, and speaks of tragedy as a *Schicksalsfabel*. But, prodded, he is willing to translate Fate as any necessary chain of events; in a word, as inevitability.

merely present their hero as is, or perhaps sketch in a few drives which may "explain" the action. Of course, there always remains the question of where the drives originate, but here too, both parties can easily be accommodated.

This uncertainty between free will and necessity can sometimes prove troublesome to the author. George Eliot, by her peculiar training and position in the intellectual and moral world, seems to have been caught at least once between the two doctrines. Her Maggie, in *The Mill on the Floss,* is swept away by her illicit passion for Stephen; on an impulse she elopes with him, and fatally injures her moral sense as a result—"she had let go the clue of life." Is Maggie responsible; i.e., was her decision to elope a free one? Eliot is of course deeply committed to an affirmative answer; and yet her own heroine appears to have puzzled her. With characteristic honesty, she asks (in Book VII, ch. 2) what can be done if a passion overwhelms, if it cannot be resisted? Is it still guilty? And she discovers no solution. Doubt now rises in us. Has Maggie's action been free, or is her sin "explained" by this not-to-be-denied passion? But howsoever we answer this question, the fundamental tragic situation, the action involving a deep injury, remains untouched.

The tendency of serious literature is, on the whole, toward psychological determinism. Even authors who are explicitly or (by their avowed Christianity) implicitly devoted to spontaneity are careful to entertain no freaks. On the contrary, they plant their motives with as much care as the sociologist, so that they would fall an easy prey—while looking the other way—to determinists, if it were not for the chink to which they can always lay claim. But at best, free will in good literature is a laced and pinched affair: we always dislike surprises in a man's actions, i.e., actions for which we find no "sufficient" causes. Corneille's Cinna, who has raged at Auguste in Act II, suddenly appears in Act III troubled and pacified, and we never know why. The father in Lessing's *Emilia Galotti* decides to murder his daughter rather than her ravisher, leaving us annoyed and astonished. In Schiller's *Rie Räuber,* a whole band of outlaws suddenly fall on their knees, and become the ministers of God! Worst of all are the psychological somersaults of Hardy, and he the most resolute determinist of all! Angel Clare, free-thinker, rebel against his father and all tradition, determinist and radical, no sooner hears that Tess was once violated than he hurries away to Brazil, casting off his bride of a few hours without a second thought. This is fine irony, and might very well represent the very extreme of freedom of the will—but it is bad art. Dryden's Lisideius, in *An Essay of Dramatic Poesy*, correctly blames plays that "end with a conversion, or simple change of will," though he does it with a sweeter temper than it deserves.

Still, as long as the author does not disagreeably surprise us, we allow him to disregard the solid chain of cause and effect. In *The Rime of the Ancient Mariner*, for example, the fatal shooting of the albatross represents, as R. P. Warren has shown, the inexplicable and motiveless appearance of sin; and in Camus' *Caligula* this noble monster (who is one of the few tragic heroes to measure up to Schlegel's demand for "inward infinite aspirations") realizes his freedom on an impulse. "*Je viens de comprendre enfin l'utilité du pouvoir. Il donne ses chances à l'impossible. Aujourd'hui, et pour tout le temps qui va venir, ma liberté n'a plus de frontières*" (1, 5).[2] Existentialist tragedy is based on the free act—*l'acte gratuit*—and the Ancient Mariner, for that matter, makes an excellent Gidean prototype.

Rather than pursue an idle course of inquiry in the gradations from absolute lack of motivation to the most minute "accounting" of an action, we will name in conclusion a few tragedies in which freedom is ruled out, and the compulsion is all within.

We find these cases in psychological studies such as *Sons and Lovers*, or cases of ignorance like that of Gide's Gertrude, in *Symphonie Pastorale*—persons who do not even know that they are impelled at all. But better still are tragedies of overwhelming passion. An overwhelming passion is never free; indeed, it is not only beyond control in its inception and its course, but it often moves against the agent's will or better judgment. The old opposition of reason and passion is that of free will and loss of control. And yet, the passions make wonderful tragedies. Phèdre, Werther, Alfieri's Mirra, Atala, to mention no others, are all

2 "At last I understand the use of power. It gives the impossible a chance. Today and for all time, my freedom is limitless."

faultlessly tragic figures; and all are carried away to their destruction by a flood which is not less irresistible because it rushes from within the soul. Such passions are a disease. Atala, caught between two irresistible forces within herself, obeys her oath of chastity only to be consumed by her passion for Chactas, and then gives in to Chactas to be destroyed by her oath. Phèdre's helplessness is well known; Hardy's Boldwood, and many other protagonists in his novels, are blinded and *unwilled* by their loves. Antony cannot free himself no matter how he rattles the chains. And what of Goriot's furious love—did he *choose* to dote on his inadequate daughters?

Finally *Othello*. The tragic action is the murder of Desdemona. Shakespeare devotes some of the greatest scenes he ever composed to a minute explanation of how Iago robbed Othello of all private will, and made him the real puppet of his own evil will, "practising upon his peace and quiet/Even to madness." Here Iago is as potent and *irresistible* a manipulator as any Greek god. His power is hypnotic: where he points, there the hapless Othello, bereft of control and judgment, goes.

"The human being," writes Volkelt, "who is blindly impelled by drives and affections, and he who is the slave of his desires and appetites, is weak of will and unfree; and still there is in this an inordinately favorable setting for tragedy." [3] It turns out that as long as we can mourn for others, whether they be free or not, we shall not find ourselves incapable of writing or understanding tragedy.

3 Volkelt, p. 147.

17 · Guilt

WELL BEYOND the "tragic flaw" is tragic guilt, of which notable examples can be found long before Aristotle wrote; and that a criminal as well as a saint can be the protagonist of a tragedy illustrates the flexibility of the genre.

Under what conditions does a sinful action become tragic? The answer is, above all, that it must be undertaken by a person who "commands our earnest good will." We must keep in mind that tragedy concerns a suffering which we deplore at least partly: the hero therefore must command sufficient approval to make us feel that there is evil when he suffers. As we saw in an earlier section, such a statement leaves a number of works open to controversy. *Richard* III is a familiar example, and Racine's *Athalie* another. Those who feel a certain admiration and therefore a liking for those personages will feel compassion as they fall. *For them,* these works fulfill our requirement of "earnest good will," whence they may be acceptable (if they fulfill the other requirements) as real tragedies. Most cases, however, appeal to the values that we all hold in common, and therefore occasion no controversy. We all know that Dr. Faustus, though he should not have made his contract with the devil, was an admirable man. And though we may take Lear for a malefactor or a fool, we know that he is worth our pity. Thus, the downfall of noble sinners is always partly saddening.

Guilt tragedies are of many kinds and degrees; but they all require that the action which is called guilty bring about inevitably, like all other tragic actions, some great pain for the actor. Allmers' egotistic life in *Little Eyolf*, Rebecca's crime in *Rosmersholm*, or Nekhlyudov's immorality in Tolstoy's *Resurrection*, all of which might have brought no pain on the actors if some external agency had not provoked feelings of remorse, are not in our sense tragic. They are paratragic intrigues.

Since guilt is a judgment brought against an action, we may ask who in tragedy judges, and who feels judged. Sometimes the judgment of guilt is only in the author's mind; that is to say, he shows his actor committing a crime without the moral awareness which he as author possesses. Raskolnikov, in *Crime and Punishment*, is a perfect example of this. The moral interest of the book is in the expectation, held up almost to the end, of Raskolnikov's recognition of his guilt. Curiously, however, his fall does not consist in that recognition, as it does in most guilt tragedies. On the contrary, the recognition of his guilt marks his rebirth. His tragic fall is the realization or consciousness of his spinelessness, his inability to reach the stature of the superman. His crime had been a test to discover whether "he had it in him" to be an unruffled *Ubermensch*. It turns out, however, that he is nervous, fearful, horrified: the test brings about a failure inevitable in the light of his character; and Raskolnikov hates himself for having an uncontrollable conscience, for suffering so fiercely from his crime. This combination of horror over the crime and the hatred of that horror constitutes his downfall. Only when he ceases to hate his remorse—when he recognizes and admits that he sinned—does he begin to revive. Throughout, Raskolnikov asserts his innocence in philosophical terms; but Dostoievsky's judgment lies upon him.

On the other hand, the judgment of guilt can be in the protagonist's mind without being in the mind of the author. Hamlet may well be an instance of this. Do we feel that Shakespeare condemns Hamlet's delay or his character, or is not Hamlet's self-revilement purely personal? A less questionable instance is that of *Lord Jim*, where the author by no means shares in the hero's feeling that he has committed a *real* and abominable crime. Paphnuce, in France's *Thaïs*, is another ex-

ample. In general, skeptics are perfectly capable of writing
tragedies of guilt, since they do not have to share their heroes'
judgment.

Further, of course, both hero and author may know and
condemn the hero's guilt. Alfieri's Mirra is consumed by a
criminal love for her father: both she and the author share in
their horror of this passion; at least, we assume this from comments of others in the play. Macbeth is in the same condition—
horror precedes and accompanies the action on all sides. The
Wilmots, in Lillo's *Fatal Curiosity*, are made on the same
model. Adam in *Paradise Lost* is of one mind with Milton; and
so is Lancelot with Tennyson in the *Idylls*.

The fact that guilt may be in the mind of the protagonist
without being in that of the author or reader creates a range of
guilt tragedies concerned with actors who are as lovable as those
in "innocent" tragedies. Sometimes the hero commits a crime
without knowing it, like Gertrude in *Symphonie Pastorale*, or
like Oedipus. (Gertrude's "crime" we take to be the dissension
she unwittingly causes in the Pastor's family; she is a siren
without knowing it.) Sometimes the hero suffers remorse where
we feel he has done no harm, or not enough at any rate to
warrant his misery: thus Lord Jim; and Alissa in *La Porte
Etroite*. Yet these are incontestable tragedies.

The reader, finally, may form a third party to these proceed-
ings, in cases where the writer fails to rally him to his own
point of view. It is quite possible, for example, for a writer to
attempt a tragedy of guilt and to fail because he cannot arouse
any sympathy for the peccant hero. What happens more frequently is that the reader excuses where the author accuses.
Many a sinner against sex taboos in Victorian narratives,
hounded to despair and death by his or her virtuous creator, has
earned the sympathy of the twentieth-century reader. Perhaps
the most notable example is that of Anna Karenina. The reader
today finds it hard to share Tolstoy's condemnation of her act
—a condemnation which, in any event, is made half-heartedly.
Too, he seems to force desolation and disaster on her, as
Dickens does on Emily in *David Copperfield*. We are in many

ways further removed from the nineteenth century than from Pericles' or Aristotle's Athens. The result may sometimes be that a writer has created tragedy without knowing it, having meant to show the nontragic fall of a leering blackguard. We are here on the borderline of tragedy, where shifts in moral sentiment disturb the referability of any definition.

18 · Inner Conflict·Dilemma·Continuous Tragedy

A] THE DIVISION between guilt (or error) and innocence is only one of a number of possible lines along which the tragic purpose may be divided. Another noteworthy division depends on the internal or external location of the antagonist. The word "antagonist" is used here in its loosest possible meaning, for it must be understood that he or it is far from being necessarily evil. The antagonist is simply that element in the original configuration whose presence causes the hero's suffering or fall.

There are two types of tragedy according to this division. In the first—the tragedy of inner conflict—the purpose is opposed by some value within the person. Paul, in *Sons and Lovers*, cannot love a woman without meeting in his own brain the tortured face of his mother, and he cannot submit to his mother without thwarting his need for a normal affection. Phaedra loves Hippolytus, but she outrages her own sense of righteousness. In Goethe's *Iphigenia in Tauris*, the heroine must lie in order to obtain her freedom and that of Orestes and Pylades. Here too, the desire for freedom meets as its antagonist an internal condition, the desire for probity. Bradley suggests that "other things being equal, the more nearly the contending forces approach each other in goodness, the more tragic is the conflict"; [1] which is true if we substitute "moving" for "tragic"—but "other things" are never equal, and while the two forces in *Iphigenia* are in almost exact balance, the play is too placid to move us nearly as much as other plays though they be stocked with villains.

[1] Bradley, "Hegel's Theory of Tragedy," p. 90.

In the second sort of tragedy, the purpose is thwarted or taxed by the existence of a person, force, condition, or fact which is external to the hero. One of the most characteristic antagonists in modern tragedies is a hostile social group or "climate," like that which defeats Hauptmann's weavers, Emma Bovary, Dr. Stockmann in *An Enemy of the People*, Brand, or Meredith's Beauchamp. Brand, for instance, is an early Gregers who tries to impose his "Nothing or else All" on the people, and naturally fails. His purpose is thwarted by an impossibility he meets in human society, not by an inner conflict.

b] All tragedies in which the purpose is consciously and voluntarily carried out are potentially tragedies of dilemma, whether the antagonist be located without or within. For the hero, in such cases, might conceivably choose not to act. In actuality, however, most tragic heroes carry out their purpose without much hesitation. The choice exists, but they do not experience it as a dilemma. An ideal illustration is Dr. Stockmann, who is made a comic personage by a happy whim on Ibsen's part, but who could be turned into a modern Prometheus with hardly a change in the text. Stockmann drives impetuously toward his goal, heedless of warnings and threats. Yet the danger to himself and to his family could easily be turned to account to create one horn of a dilemma. Hernani, in Hugo's play, might have hesitated between love and honor, and Antigone between religion and state, but their fanatical virtue dissolves the dilemma before it can crystallize.

Hesitation, then, creates the dilemma, and tragedies of this kind have a peculiar fascination, at the opposite pole of the tragedies of single-mindedness, of overwhelming passion, of instinct, and of ignorance. Here we find Goethe's Iphigenia again, torn between probity and love of her brother, Paul Morel between mother and mistress, Grillparzer's Medea between father and lover, Titus between Bérénice and Rome, Alissa between God and Jérôme, Adam between uxorious love and obedience to God, and countless others.

The tragic dilemma has often been the means to present and discuss an ethical problem. The French classicists took much delight in elegant quandaries, and maneuvered their characters into the most fantastic postures for the sake of a puzzle. Nor has the dilemma lost favor in our times; but it has been purged for better or for worse of French artificiality. From the dramatization it was then of fine questions concerning love and honor made for perfumed disputes in a salon (a pastime which had amused these very ladies' medieval ancestors), the dilemma has become in the hands of serious writers the opportunity to exercise the soul on the gravest issues, and reveal the world's most exquisite cruelties.

It is in this species of tragedy that we are most likely to find without equivocation an affirmation of man's nobility. Here man is tempted into cowardly happiness, safe decrepitude, or sinful ease, and overcomes the temptation though often at the price of his very life. But now, when he dies, we may well be asked to exult. Achilles will not rest at home; Prometheus will not purchase relief from Zeus; Aeneas will not loll in Carthage; the saint will not sacrifice to Jupiter; the soldier will not cower in his trench. Man is glorified, and suffering consciously accepted glorifies him. To be sure, he may be exalted for opposite qualities: the glory of Racine's Titus is that he yields love to the state; the glory of Dryden's Antony is that he yields the state to love; but no matter—both plays affirm the greatness of man.

All we must remember is that this is but one kind of tragedy. For even in the tragedy of dilemma, it may happen that the virtuous choice turns to evil and disappointment. Having chosen, the hero may recognize in the end that he mistook evil for good; or his pain may be so outrageous that he curses the good; or virtue may itself carry a germ of sin which tortures the hero. This is what causes the choking gloom of Graham Greene's *The Heart of the Matter*. Whatever good Scobie does burdens him with an equivalent evil. He cannot love without inflicting pain on someone else or damning his own soul. And his supreme act of love, what to many authors would provide a great major chord, is also his supreme sin: in order to stop giving pain to his wife and his mistress, he commits the mortal sin of suicide.

In a few cases, the dilemma appears as insoluble. The hero

is paralyzed, unable to act at all, except by withdrawing in final despair. It is questionable, however, whether these rare situations are fully tragic. Thus Browning's Luria, the Moorish commander of the Florentines. After his victory over the Pisans, he is torn by a dilemma: if he remains with the Florentines, he is to be tried and executed by them, for he knows that they are conspiring to destroy him. If, however, he goes over to the Pisans, he betrays all the culture and beauty for which Florence stands. As it does not occur to Browning that he could simply go away, and leave both Florentines and Pisans to their own devices, we are given here an insoluble dilemma which Luria ends by taking poison. Another example is Séleucus, in Corneille's *Rodogune*. This young man must kill his mother to gain his mistress, or kill his mistress to gain the throne (by his mother's favor). He too withdraws: *"J'éteins enfin ma flamme et mon ambition"*—"I extinguish at last my love and my ambition" (III, 5).

The first case is not tragic because death here is both the action and the downfall; whereas it is manifest that downfall must *follow* from an action, that is to say from something other than itself. The second case—withdrawal—offers a *solution* for the tragic dilemma. The protagonist discovers that he does not need to act at all. It goes without saying that a work which presents a purpose in the midst of a tragic configuration, and then cheats us by simply canceling the purpose, is not likely to be a masterpiece.

But withdrawal can itself be one of the horns of the dilemma. It can be the tragic purpose. Indeed, we speak of tragic purpose rather than tragic action, not only because the hero may never "exteriorize" his wish (and yet suffer), but also because inaction can be purposeful and tragic. Hamlet, for example, does not simply collapse like Séleucus. He purposefully rejects action because action in a chaotic world is vain and futile. But this refusal is tragic—not because of the rigmarole by which Shakespeare finally cuts short the play, but because of the suffering inaction entails—"O! what a rogue and peasant slave am I."

c] The other reason for keeping to the word "purpose" is that some tragedies do not have any action at all except perhaps some climactic gesture. There is, in other words, a tragedy of unutterable motive, where both purpose and agony are silent and concealed. We shall find this again and again in the stories of guilty passions: Mirra's, and, in Chateaubriand's *René*, Amélie's incestuous loves find no vent in action, in contrast to the loves of Giovanni and Annabella (*'Tis Pity She's a Whore*) or Siegfried and Sieglinde. The two heroines burn in silence. Atala, after a long paroxysm of silence, does act; and so does Phaedra, her French sister Phèdre, and Werther, though the last three only by expressing in words what lay hidden. Their tragedies, nonetheless, have been mute torment of the soul. Paphnuce in *Thaïs* also gets ground down in speechless and inactive solitude; and Alissa in *La Porte Etroite* pours out her passion no further than her diary.

This leads us to another division of tragic purposes. The purpose or action may be a single event, or it may be continuous. In the cases we have just seen, and most other passions, the action and its punishment are incessant. There are a great many tragedies of this sort: we may name the episode in *Morte D'Arthur* dealing with the fair maid of Astolat, or Kafka's *Das Schloss*, or d'Annunzio's *La Gloria*. In the latter, for instance, Ruggero Flamma is continuously driven by his ambition into excesses which horrify and finally kill him. Père Goriot is another and perfect example. His life is one long passion for his daughters, and that passion is constantly rebuffed by the very excess of its demands. Eugénie Grandet also loves in silence for many years, and suffers continuously besides. These tragedies are among the most painful and constricting of the genre, and it is a relief to the reader when the suffering hero finally dies. Their painfulness resembles in fact that of the works which concern themselves with victims; and we might be forgiven the error of thinking that Goriot and Eugénie are actually nothing but victims. But though they may be called "victims of their passion" they are really purposeful tragic protagonists. Their action is mental; but they seek, they crave, they persist and suffer inevitable harm as a result—they lead tragic lives; and it does not matter whether they lift their hand or not.

19 · Consciousness and Recognition

WE LIMIT ourselves here to consciousness and recognition in the tragic protagonist, and leave out of account the reader himself. The reader, of course, may be left in the dark as to the tragic purpose or the fatal configuration until late in the action; but what concerns us now is the degree of consciousness in the actor.

The definition does not pronounce on this subject; it does not require that the key action be consciously undertaken, nor that the protagonist realize anything in particular except the fact that he suffers. And yet many commentators have written as though knowledge were of the essence. The tragic hero, says Jaspers, may find deliverance through his recognition of the tragic process, "which, brought to light, can purify the mind"; the hero carries "his human possibilities to their extreme and can be undone by them with his eyes open—that is his greatness"; and further, "in struggle he becomes aware of that power for which he stands, that power which is yet not everything." [1] What distinguishes the tragic from the comic hero, says another critic, is that the tragic hero learns: he gains insight into himself and the world, and thus (like Creon and Lear) acquires humility and compassion.[2] Knowledge is usually seen as the condition of reconciliation and the final affirmation which tragedy is alleged to make: "The hero's purpose is

[1] Jaspers, pp. 43, 56, 75. We recognize, of course, that Jaspers speaks from the *parti-pris* of his philosophy.
[2] Stolnitz, *passim*.

147

defeated, his passion is harrowing, but through his final perception he comes to terms with his fate—or if he doesn't, the spectator does." [3] Recognition may have a philosophical value, as Jaspers contends, or it may be looked upon as heuristic: "The tragic hero's steadfast confrontation of his predicament stirs us . . . because we sense it might save us from such defeats as these." [4] But at this point we are close to fantasy.

If we think of knowledge or recognition exclusively in terms of the tragic purpose, and omit the recognition scenes which Aristotle discusses (e.g., Electra recognizing Orestes)—in other words, if we restrict ourselves to the *éclaircissement* of the actor concerning the true nature of all his actions at the moment of downfall—we find that tragedy offers three possibilities: *first*, the actor proceeds throughout with full lucidity, knows more or less completely what to expect, and is not surprised by his own misery; *second*, the actor proceeds with hope of success, unaware of the doom which his purpose necessarily entails, and only recognizes the truth and the horror when it is too late; and *third*, the protagonist proceeds in ignorance, suffers in ignorance, and dies in ignorance.

The first category is conscious tragedy, the second is tragedy with recognition (*anagnorisis*), the third is blind tragedy.

French neoclassical drama is largely conscious. It takes place in actual daylight and in spiritual clarity. Nature does not abhor a vacuum more than French tragedy dislikes hugger-mugger. In startling contrast, British tragedy takes place, typically, in a night both actual and spiritual. Its characters grope blindly and act spasmodically in a world whose laws they do not know, a world which perhaps has none. But they usually learn the truth before they die.

The tragedy of dilemma is, by the very nature of the case, conscious tragedy. A notable instance is that of *Billy Budd*, with its perfectly lucid Captain Vere weighing the consequences of his decision. The case is the same for his ancestress Antigone, and for all the heroes and heroines who choose. Lear and Othello, on the other hand, act blindly, but recognize the

3 Muller, p. 19.
4 Lesser, p. 136.

truth in the end. Others may not even be aware that they are acting at all. Witness the mother in Lawrence's *The Rocking-Horse Winner*. Her rapacity is almost unexpressed; Paul hears of it vaguely: the call for money is like a permanent but ghostly echo in the house. And unknown to his mother, Paul is murdering himself in order to obtain money for her. She never realizes until it is too late that her guilty purpose is tragically (because inevitably) driving Paul to his death; but then she too has her flash of recognition.

Paul himself, however, obtains no recognition at all. Ahab of *Moby Dick* does not have at his supreme moment the flashing insight that all he had labored for could never have succeeded, though ten Ahabs had banded together for the kill. The wretched K. in Kafka's *Schloss* still walks in blindness as the book closes. Regardless of whether or not he might have recognized the futility of his endeavor on his deathbed, he appears as a tragic figure even as the book stumbles to a halt. Nor does the hero of *Sons and Lovers* fully realize his trouble, even though it is an "I" narrative which reveals the truth to *us*. In a word, an author is entitled to inflict suffering on a protagonist without ever enlightening the latter as to reasons and motives.

It must be admitted that few writers are satisfied with darkness. Most of them feel that a certain degree of unveiling, a cry of "So this was how" ought to complete the beauty of the design. It is very well for a man to kill his father and marry his mother, but what if he does not even know it, and lives on merrily in ignorance? This is not tragedy, and it is difficult to see how it could be very satisfying art. At one time or another, he must realize the horror of his deeds and suffer for them. Recognition, therefore, is often the climactic point of tragedy. It adds an irony to the already scathing irony of the original tragic hope, in that knowledge, far from being a boon, may be the heaviest burden of all.

What is the precise role of recognition in the tragedies where it occurs? We must distinguish here between tragic and adventitious recognition. A tragic recognition is one which is inevitably bound up with the (blind) tragic purpose and which causes the hero's undoing, or at least contributes to it. Adventitious recognition is one which happens to follow after the tragic downfall, and thus completes the artistic or philosophic design. Essential though it may be to the design of the whole work, it is not strictly speaking a portion of the tragedy.

Both Eugénie Grandet and Père Goriot love unworthy objects for a period of many years. They suffer continuously. Thus Balzac says of Eugénie, "*Cet amour . . . ne lui causait que des douleurs mêlées de frêles espérances*"—"This love brought her only sorrow mingled with frail hopes." While poor Goriot lets his daughters "pinch him like torturers" for ten years before he dies. The profound tragic theme of both works is the same as that in Flaubert's great work, although the latter has denied his heroine the sentimental proportions that Balzac gives his. In *Père Goriot*, Rastignac states this theme: "*Comment les grands sentiments s'allieraient-ils, en effet, à une société mesquine, petite, superficielle?*"—How, after all, could great feelings be allied to a petty, small, superficial society?

Yet for a long time, both Eugénie and Goriot are uninformed. They believe that their love can and will be reciprocated ultimately. They are therefore both blind and tragic. But in both cases, Balzac reserves for them the final shock of knowledge. Eugénie knows Charles for what he is, and Goriot exclaims in his agony, just before his death, "*Je suis dupe! elles ne m'aiment pas, elles ne m'ont jamais aimé!*" Their discovery suddenly accentuates the tragic catastrophe by bringing on an emotional crisis. We may recall the somewhat similar recognition Catherine experiences in Henry James' *Washington Square*, a recognition which turns her into a spinster bearing, incidentally, a strong resemblance to Eugénie.

Turning back twenty-three centuries, we discover a contributory recognition in *Alcestis*, provided we grant that Admetus is a tragic personage. At first, he is merely disconsolate at having had to sacrifice his wife in order to preserve his own life. He has no sense of guilt or shame as yet, but he is thoroughly unhappy. Only when he returns from the burial does he realize suddenly that "I, I who should have died, I have escaped my fate. . . . Only now do I perceive it." And further: "Those who hate me will say: 'See how he lives in shame, the man who dared not die, the coward who gave his wife to Hades in his stead! Is

that a man?' " Again, the protagonist's suffering is made acute
by the recognition of the truth—in this case, a recognition of
guilt; but he had shed tears even in his blindness.

The classical instance is, of course, *Karamazov*. In the shadowy
world of half-consciousness, Ivan has willed his father's death
by his purposive, hence tragic, inaction. The tragic shock comes
to him when the actual murder brings home to his consciousness the dreadful truth of his responsibility, and, like Oedipus,
he knows himself the criminal. Intelligence overthrows Ivan.

Sometimes, however, recognition is the sole cause and agent
of the overthrow. If Theseus in Euripides' *Hippolytus* had not
realized that the son he had killed was innocent, he would have
continued satisfied. In Otway's *The Orphan*, Polydore does not
scruple to ravish Monimia; only when he discovers that she is
his brother's wife does he despair. Recognition is equally essential in Ibsen's *Little Eyolf*. The tragic action here is Allmers'
whole way of life before the play opens—specifically, his indulgence of the self, his sexual acquisitiveness, the evil of which
is symbolized by the crippled child. Now Allmers lives on
prosperously enough until his wife forces him to recognize the
guilt of his ways. At that moment he collapses.

Actually, tragedies in which the downfall depends exclusively
on recognition are fairly uncommon, for it is difficult to make
recognition inevitable. Occasionally, to be sure, we meet with a
situation in which an action undertaken in blindness will have
to be recognized. Lear's foolish act of land distribution bears
the inevitable fruit not only of disaster for him, but recognition
of the error as well. Heracles, explicitly maddened only long
enough to massacre his family, will have to wake up and see.
Deianeira, who unwittingly sends Heracles a poisoned robe (in
Trachiniae) must hear that the robe killed her husband. In *The
Fatal Curiosity* (Lillo) old Wilmot kills a stranger; but since in
the original configuration several people are aware of the young
man's identity, it is inevitable that Wilmot will recognize him
as his son. Finally, the inevitable result of Eve's sin, in *Paradise
Lost*, is not only expulsion from the garden, but the awareness
of her guilt as well.

But more frequently, the original configuration does not
necessarily involve recognition. Eugénie might never have dis-

covered what a rascal Charles had turned out to be, and the un-
deceiving of Othello is by no means to be deduced from the
murder of his wife. Admetus need not necessarily have discovered his guilt; and more certainly still, Theseus might have
remained forever in ignorance of his son's purity.

Wherever a contingent recognition is merely the climax of a
tragedy, or an additional source of suffering, tragedy is unim-
paired. Where, however, a contingent recognition is also essential to the overthrow, there is a certain shortcoming in the work,
at least from the point of view of tragedy. We are again in the
realm of paratragic rather than tragic literature: since recognition might not have occurred, the hero might not have fallen.
The purest tragedies are those in which the climactic recognition is not essential to the overthrow, where it is only one of
the contributory "accidents," tending in an already established
direction.

It is edifying to see how Racine improved on Euripides in
this respect. In Euripides' play, Theseus has cursed and killed
his son, and he contemplates his deed with the satisfaction of a
job well done. Answering the Messenger who has brought news
of Hippolytus' death, all he says is, "My hatred for him who
hath thus suffered made me glad at thy tidings, yet from regard
for the gods and him, because he is my son, I feel neither joy
nor sorrow at his suffering." Then suddenly Artemis appears,
and carefully recounts to Theseus the events as they really
happened. *Only then* is Theseus struck low. Thus, recognition
overthrows him, but that recognition, that overthrow, were not
inevitable.

Racine has bettered his model. For even as Thésée launches
his curse, he is troubled and unhappy:

> *Je t'aimais; et je sens que malgré ton offense*
> *Mes entrailles pour toi se troublent par avance.*
> (IV, iii.)[5]

The casual machinery by which Thésée discovers his error becomes here a contributory accident, and does not impair the

---

5 "I loved you; and my bowels are stirred for you already, in spite of
your offense." Actually, Racine took a hint from Seneca, whose Theseus
is also aggrieved at the moment when he learns that Hippolytus is dead.

tragedy at all; whereas Euripides' Theseus, dependent for his overthrow entirely on the *deux ex machina*, makes at best only a quasi-tragic figure.

In general, then, writers have found that an inevitable recognition is hard to get. And in general, inevitable or otherwise, they have preferred allowing recognition merely to cap their stories, and to afford the crisis to an already existing tragedy. We have mentioned the ignorant mother in *The Rocking-Horse Winner*. It is inevitable that she lose her son: and this is the tragedy for her. It is not inevitable, but most fitting, that she should also discover that her guilt killed him. Guinevere's adultery in the *Idylls of the King* inevitably undermines and corrupts the Round Table (in fact, we can read the story as that of another Fall). It is not inevitable, though highly desirable, that Guinevere come to grief by recognizing her own evil. On the other hand, Racine's Oreste kills Hermione's lover Pyrrhus at her own order, not realizing that she still loves Pyrrhus. *His* first tragedy is the remorse he feels over the murder itself; his second, climactic tragedy is his recognition that Hermione still loves Pyrrhus, and that she will now hate him, Oreste, more than ever. This second recognition-overthrow, unlike the former examples, is inevitable, and yet it too only adds to a pre-existent catastrophe.

It is the particular glory of Sophocles that consciously or unconsciously he recognized the trap of quasi-tragedy for his *Oedipus* and travelled clear of it. He carefully did not write a play on "How Oedipus unwittingly slew his father and married his mother, and on discovering his double crime blinded himself"; for how, if not through a clumsy Euripidean god acting as an information bureau, would Oedipus have discovered his guilt? How could an author achieve an inevitable recognition? Avoiding the artistic error, Sophocles adopted a better theme: "How Oedipus, searching for the murderer of Laius, and his own identity, discovered his double crime as a result." He wrote a tragedy on recognition itself, a feat which has not often been repeated.

With recognition, we see once more how art may transform and beautifully falsify life. Actually, it is not at all likely that a Père Goriot, at the end of a cruel life, should suddenly understand the ravaging truth; nor that a blind beggar should pass by Madame Bovary's window and reveal to her the meaning of her death. Any blame of *Madame Bovary* for "ruthless realism" must be in error, for the work is in fact a formal Greek perfection in defiance of life, terribly real in one sense and yet unreally harmonious in all its parts. Authors find an almost irresistible need to amend the shocking disregard of nature for *completion*. That a child should suffer and die moves us enough; that it should suffer and die quite unrecorded and unknown in a forgotten corner is almost intolerable. And in the same fashion, the author is loath to trouble and torture his protagonists, and then allow them to die without even the small saving grace of knowing who or what struck them to earth. Ignorance bears with it the persistent urge to make light, just as the fingers hovering over an indecisive discord on the keyboard long to resolve it. That the discord need not be resolved modern music has proved, and literature has done as well. But one of the tendencies of our nature is still to complete what is incomplete, and therefore the voice still comes to the suffering hero, making his life, if not happy, at least intelligible.

Let us recapitulate: 1] Some tragic heroes are lucid throughout. 2] Some are blind throughout. In neither of these cases does recognition occur. 3] Some tragedies end in recognition, and this recognition causes the downfall. 4] Some tragedies end in recognition, but recognition only contributes to the downfall. 5] Paratragedies are works of the third category in which recognition is accidental, not inevitable. With this summary, we mark the place of consciousness in tragic literature, and reassert that the fact of tragedy does not hang on its presence or its absence.

20 · The Suffering Hero

TRAGEDY demands suffering. All suffering is spiritual, of course, but sometimes the source of pain is so emphatically actual torture of the flesh that we may be justified in naming it separately. The most outstanding example of "pure" physical agony is Prometheus. On the moral side, his triumph is absolute. But he pays heavily in bodily pain, and he does not scorn pain.

Actually, no physical disorder is in itself necessarily frightful. Individuals can always be found who will endure or even welcome it. Death especially can be thought an actual improvement in one's condition. Who would not be relieved to see the hero of *Farewell to Arms* die; who does not feel that *at last* Lear is laid to rest? For the most painful stories are often those in which the sufferers cannot die. And this is why in the final analysis physical pain must be translated into psychological terms—must, in other words, be hated—before it can make a tragedy. This is also why we are forced to speak of doubtful tragedies whenever we are not sure that the protagonist really suffers. The question is often proposed concerning *Samson Agonistes*. All the conditions for tragedy seem to be present:

> Each Philistian City round
> Met from all parts to solemnize this Feast.
> Samson with these immixt, inevitably
> Pull'd down the same destruction on himself.
> (1655–1658)

Of course we do not see Samson in his last moments; but does he suffer at all, or is not his death an unmitigated victory? Manoa thinks the latter:

155

Nothing is here for tears, nothing to wail,
Or knock the breast, no weakness, no contempt,
Dispraise, or blame, nothing but well and fair,
And what may quiet us in a death so noble.
                                    (1721–1724)

The poem in its final pages breathes nothing but noble resolution. It seems to be closer to *An Enemy of the People* than to *Prometheus Bound*. True, Milton does not give us any positive information about Samson's ultimate feelings, so that we may if we wish imagine that Samson has not left the world without deep regret. But this view does not harmonize with the tone of the last pages, and it conflicts with Samson's reiterated expressions of disgust with life.

A less doubtful and a notable case is Addison's Cato of the "high, unconquered heart." Heaven's inflictions, says this inflexible hero, give man occasion to exert his virtue and hidden strength. His tragic or paratragic action is the decision not to surrender to Caesar, and not to compromise with evil. Or we may say that the action is his refusal to fly to safety; he will keep an heroic virtue by remaining in Rome and dying. But does Cato mind dying? Apparently not. He reminds us rather of the Socrates who expires so willingly in the *Phaedo*. Socrates can extricate himself from the sentence by various undignified and dubious means. There is what looks like a dilemma between unrighteousness and life on one side and righteousness with death on the other. As it turns out, however, the second alternative, which would appear uncomfortable to most people, does not seem in the least objectionable to Socrates. Righteousness is good, but death is not ill: "Those of us who think that death is an evil are in error." Hence his choice entails no evil, and is not tragic. He dies with the utmost serenity.[1] Both his and Cato's are pseudo-dilemmas.

More recently, we meet with T. S. Eliot's Thomas Becket, in *Murder in the Cathedral*, who allows himself to be run through more willingly, even, than Polyeucte:

1 The death of Christ, as we have seen, is anguished and tempestuous. Montaigne has a whole list of instances of persons who go to their deaths without minding. (See I, 14, "*Que le Goust des Biens et des Maux Dépend en Bonne Partie de l'Opinion que Nous en Avons.*")

> all things
> Proceed to a joyful consummation.

God has chosen him to be a martyr for the sake of God's Law as against man's equity as well as man's inequity, for the sake of the timeless as against the temporal, and for the sake of Christ in atonement for His suffering. Although the play is admirable in several respects, in others it is rather crude compared to *The Cocktail Party*. For example, the representation of evil is refined, in the later play, to include not only the brutality of murder but also the civilized *malaise* which results from a vacuum in the soul. More germanely to our present subject, Celia, the heroine of *The Cocktail Party*, suffers, in the process of her exaltation, the "reluctance of the body to become a *thing*"—in Mr. Eliot's magnificent phrase. This reluctance, this horror, is simply missing as a dimension in Thomas' character. He may be the better saint therefor; but he is not, for better or for worse, a tragic hero.

In short, tragedy does not deal with unflinching heroes, Achilles without heels. A man so tough, and, we might add, so monomaniacal that no harm can touch him is not a tragic hero. The tales in which he figures are, if he happens to represent our own view of the world, the noblest and the most bracing. Tragedy is pitched a little lower: it is above all an account of human suffering, from which these nonpareils are excluded. They die, but they are too calm, while tragedy demands,

> if calm at all,
> If any calm, a calm despair.

21 · The Post-tragic Episodes

IN A PREVIOUS section, we saw that recognition often occurs after the tragedy has been consummated. In an earlier section, we noted that tragedy is not necessarily coterminous with the work of art as a whole. The post-tragic episodes have a place in this inquiry because they may carry us back to the tragedy itself, and make the final emotional or philosophical commentary on the action. It is here, rather than in the tragic action itself, that we may on occasion find an uplift, a reconciliation, or on the other side a final push into the abyss. Some authors may wish to re-establish a certain serenity of mood, others to offer an intellectual promise after the downfall, still others to end in redoubled negation.

Shakespeare's tragedies tend to conclude in a somewhat sobering manner, but the final speeches are, for most readers, not "heavy" enough to make a substantial change in emotional or intellectual atmosphere. There are more instructive instances: Milton could have presented the tragedy of *Paradise Lost* as an unpalliated calamity. Instead, he sends off his two sinners with a blessing, long hopeful speeches, and some movingly serene last lines.[1] Eugénie Grandet is followed into her later melan-

1 This, at any rate, is the usual verdict. For others, and myself among them, the last two books of *Paradise Lost* are singularly dispiriting. Milton forces Adam to rejoice over a historical pageant of horrors which should have stunned him. History, unfortunately, gave Milton no alternative. Cervantes offers a more plausible consolation in *La Numancia* to the Spaniards defeated by Scipio Aemilianus: the Spirit of the river Duero predicts that, centuries later, it will be the Spaniards' turn to conquer Rome.

choly but peaceful years. Hardy's *Woodlanders* ends with the beautiful and serene picture of Marty South's solitary watch over Giles Winterbourne's tomb.[2] In *Wuthering Heights* Heathcliff peacefully achieves his reunion with Catherine. *Hippolytus, John Gabriel Borkmann, Polyeucte,* Hauptmann's *Michael Kramer* and a great number of other works conclude with some kind of reconciliation (though the protagonist is dead), while others, like *Germinal* and *The Idylls of the King,* strike a note of hope for the future.

But reconciliation, submission, resignation, the attainment of peace, do not necessarily affect the reader's *intellectual* response. Seeing the sisters reconciled over Borkmann's body, hearing Swinburne's Meleager forgive his mother for having murdered him, or listening to Maurya's fervent resignation does not give us any important new intellectual vision besides inducing the idea that peace of mind is a possible thing after calamity. Of course, the post-tragic episodes may be, or contain, a philosophic commentary on the protagonist's fall, and as such dictate our view of the matter; but usually, these quiet final scenes are meant to be emotionally rather than intellectually soothing.

On the other hand, the author may seize upon the post-tragic period to add salt to the wound. We find such manipulations, among other places, in *Oedipus,* where the hero has to abandon his children as he goes into exile; in *Goriot,* where the daughters fail to appear at the funeral, and in *A Lear of the Steppes,* where both daughters prosper after their crime.

The strongest form which post-tragic restoration can take is the redemption of the protagonist. This must be distinguished from the moral victory which constitutes one side of the tragedy itself—that, say, of Antigone or Isabel Archer in James's novel. We are concerned here with a victory which follows the downfall without being inevitably bound up with it. While such a victory may be essential to the design as a whole, it is a discrete

---

Incidentally, at the end of this play occurs another common form of post-tragic consolation, namely the promise of being remembered forever:
From Bactria to Thule, from one pole to the other,
a promise which sweetens many a defeat and death in ancient literature.

2 A scene reminiscent of the close of Turgenev's *Fathers and Sons.*

event whose omission would not impair the tragic nature of the work. An obvious instance is the *Oresteia*. The tragedy occurs when Orestes is pursued by the Furies as a result of his matricide. Later the gods redeem him. Their mansuetude is of course a vital part of the trilogy; it gives Aeschylus' interpretation of the legend, and it colors our intellectual and emotional apprehension of the tragedy itself. We might have felt indignation as Orestes fell, while now we are mollified and restored. We return in our imagination to the critical moment when Orestes first felt madness come upon him, and we see his misery in a new light. But for all this, Orestes' rehabilitation, like the other post-tragic episodes, is only a chapter after the tragedy.

The redemption of Orestes is echoed in all the characteristic Christian tragedies. Guilty heroes, having been cast down materially or spiritually by their sins, repent and are saved. Innocent heroes who have suffered martyrdom are carried aloft into heaven and rewarded. Even before that, the wounds that they have received in defense of the faith may be healed by angels, as we read in the legend of Saint Catherine. Nevertheless, these stories are tragic; that is to say, the tragedy is consummated, regardless of what follows after.[3] Only if the angels interfered in time to prevent any suffering would tragedy be averted.

Some post-tragic redemptions in literature are fairly shallow and perhaps regrettable: Rodrigue's fortunate turn, after he has had to kill Chimène's father; or Maggie Tulliver's reunion in death with her brother, after her great sin. Frequently, however, redemption is a deeply satisfying return on the tragic narrative: *Crime and Punishment*, *Lord Jim* are good examples; and, as Professor Jebb explains, so is Sophocles' *Ajax*. The long dispute which follows Ajax's suicide, whether he is to be buried or not, has as its real issue whether Ajax shall be abandoned as a sinner, or whether he shall be considered rehabilitated. His final inhumation is his victory. Then there are old legends about Judas which portray his eventual return to Christ's arms, thus providing an ultimate blessing even to that tragedy. Goethe's *Faust*, of course, is an account of two redemptions, and so is *The Scarlet Letter*. In Hauptmann's *Kaiser Karls Geisel*,

3 See the passage on Christ's Passion in section 14.

Charlemagne, after a temporary and tragic infatuation with the lawless Gersuind, returns to statescraft and sanity. Guinevere too, it may be remembered, dies in the odor of sanctity.

In these tales, tragedy is still perfectly realized. All the actors suffer gravely as a result of their errors and sins, but the authors, far from leaving us to solace ourselves with vague mutterings about the eternal beauty of the soul or proved nobility of character, explicitly present a cosmos in which error does not doom the protagonist forever. In *The Scarlet Letter* while Dimmesdale suffers, he suffers as much as the most miserable of the tragic heroes; but our mood may change at the end of his story, when the author seems to command joy for the redemption of a soul.

22 · Tragic Reality

THE TRAGIC IDEA on which so many works of art rest is one of the great platitudes which stagger only when we look at them as though we had never noticed them before. It is well, on the whole, that the most frightening ideas are so evident and so commonplace that they only occasionally alarm us, in the night perhaps, when we are alone, at times of great sorrow, or in certain unusual moods or situations. Yet such ideas—and their joyous counterparts too—continue to provide the raw materials for all the arts. In each generation, the artist is called upon to reword them in the idiom of the day. When he tires of them, his art becomes esoteric, mannered, decadent. The search for the altogether new, the determination to express an emotion never felt before, issues in exquisite art for the coterie. But the *outré* does not in its turn become the norm; rather it provokes another reaction, and a robust return to the undying platitudes. If it did become the norm, art would really progress, whereas of course it does no such thing. Like the clouds, whose shapes and colors are never twice the same, yet which always rise from the same natural cycle and catch the same sun, art moves from age to age through unrepeated shapes, but is always itself in essence.

The human situation which lies at the root of tragic art is thus simple, perpetual, and (when it makes itself felt) awesome. The situation is not simply that human effort fails, but that failure lies implicit in the effort. Some men—and, indeed, some cultures—are so preoccupied with their realization of this

radical shortcoming of human existence that they withdraw
from all activity and condemn the will. Others are content with
the limited successes which life offers between the two eternities
on either side of it, and, leaving death out of the problem by a
kind of daily prestidigitation, assent to a conditional optimism.
Most men are granted even better: death does not preoccupy
them at all, "they are not philosophers," and they live as
buoyantly as if they were immortal. We could call this stupidity; but it seems more like a last kindness of Nature, when she
inflicted on man the foreknowledge of his own death.

Death with its inevitable victory over effort is then the first
tragic fact. The second tragic fact is a socio-psychological one:
the very act of living in the society of others brings with it—
unavoidably, "naturally"—friction, hate, misery. The tragic purpose is the desire, or rather the need, to live among one's kind.
If the radical flaw in this desire is interpreted as the perpetua-
tion of an offense committed against God, we can speak of
original sin. Sin as the misalliance between man and man (Cain
murdering Abel) is indeed original, that is to say, essential,
built into the very fact of sociable life. Thus the act of birth is
tragic not only because it is simultaneously the condemnation
to death (so that, as we watch our newborn child, we may
fancy that we have brought another death into the world), but
also because it fastens on the child the inevitability of suffering
among his own species.

> *Pues el delito mayor*
> *Del hombre es haber nacido*

says the prince Segismundo in *La Vida Es Sueño*: the greatest
crime of man is to be born. In the universal ritual of the seasons,
the interlock of birth and death, spring and winter, fertility and
sterility, is acutely realized. Once more, the distance between
catastrophe and inevitable catastrophe is decisive. A man's crop
may be blighted by the magic spells of an enemy: that is one
thing. Quite another is the necessary blight brought by the
winter, for that one is built into the hopeful act of sowing itself.
One could not confuse the two species of event.

We meet with tragic fact at every level. We hear of the folly of being wise, which is undoubtedly a tragic notion, and of evil as the *sine qua non* of good. Some cultures, it appears, grew into their glory by means of oppression and slavery. In our own time, we look on troubled while at every leap of the day our wealth, our comfort, our control of the world increase, and a dreadful spiritual desiccation keeps pace, the shadow growing with the body. The sense of doom, which is so characteristic of contemporary art and philosophy, and penetrates even into the speeches of some public men, does not *happen* to co-exist with the material and social achievements of our times; it rose out of the very heart of success. At the point of the perfect "organization of human resources" comes the death of the soul. Eventually we ask whether the flaw does not lie at the root of every reform. How many advances, liberations, revolutions, hailed as new epochs in human affairs, are really progressions from Scylla into Charybdis? Here peons are given land, only to starve on it. There, a colonial people is set free, only to bleed in civil wars. Elsewhere patriots overthrow a tyrant to become tyrants themselves. And where is success? Is not the Stoic right when he preaches a return to the soul itself? Is not the grasping for wealth, liberty, security, and perhaps even love, self-defeating—rotten in the act itself?

These are mere suggestions, obvious enough. One does not have to subscribe to them *in toto* to feel how tragic art naturally emerges out of life's own conditions. Historical tragedies, in which the protagonist is a nation or an entire civilization, strike us with especial force. Nothing is so melancholy as a study of Europe since the Industrial Revolution. We read here powerful tragedies of guilt and good intentions, classic in all their lines. Logically, but only logically, the new capitalists of the nineteenth century had two ways open to them. They could disregard the notions of justice entertained in theory by most Europeans, and ride roughshod over the masses of people who were now in their hands; or they could create a system of distribution by which they would restrict their own wealth but satisfy the proletariat and the natives in the colonies, and at the same time glut the world with riches. Needless to say, the capitalists, in the image of the feudal landlords who preceded them, took the luxurious alternative of driving their slaves to the uttermost. This continuous act of guilt (we are dealing with a continuous tragedy enacted in reality) bore as its necessary consequences the class wars and the colonial revolutions of our own day. That the downtrodden should get the better of it was by no means certified in the original configuration; but the tragedy was consummated, regardless of its outcome, in the terrors, miseries and massacres of the last generations.

No less tragic has been the social upheaval in itself. Here too we recognize without difficulty a tragic purpose: call it the longing for social justice, though a better name for it is the natural greed of the dispossessed. In Shelley's times a gentleman might foresee a noble unchaining of the Outraged People, whether Greeks against Turks or British mill workers against Gradgrinds. We know better (as the Romans who had survived Marius knew better) what a rising of the people, however just in itself, brings to the world in new miseries, dictatorship by demagogues, civil and international wars, fresh spoliations and unforeseen oppressions, and, as always, the butchery of the innocent. Such are not adventitious but altogether inevitable consequences of these upheavals; there are no clean revolutions. Tough theory-makers proclaim that the end justifies the means—a tragic concept: blood *must* be shed as we march to the City of God.[1]

Historical tragedy has its counterpart in the tragedy of historical figures—of leaders whose leadership necessarily miscarried and drove men in directions other than they had imagined. Christ did not live to see the havoc wrought by, and the perversions imposed on, his doctrines; but Ghandi witnessed the slaughter which was released by the very act of independence in India, and Chamberlain lived long enough to see the unavoidable bankruptcy of his well-meant policies. We may count it an axiom, which leaders of mankind unfortunately ignore, that in every great movement—religious or social—success means failure, popularity is corruption, the triumph of purity is the end of purity.

1 In a remarkable scene of *Point Counterpoint*, Aldous Huxley denounces any millenium which depends on the murder of even one vile person. The same problem occurs, of course, in Dostoievsky.

While great men make impressive tragic figures, we meet with tragic situations at every turn among the mass of mankind. We are all acquainted with cases of sacrifice for the "greater good"—say the relinquishment of pleasure for the sake of religion, of love for the sake of a parental tie, of life for the sake of the fatherland. We may observe, with regard to the last instance, that propagandists do not usually present the patriot's conscious self-sacrifice with a tragic emphasis; they neglect the pain for the exaltation of death, the danger for them, in the tragic view, being that it is a wonderful moderator of fanaticism and enthusiasm. Such is the picture we have of those Japanese warriors who, we are told, crashed with their planes on a target out of single-minded patriotism. And it is incontestably true that fanatics do not make tragic figures.

Some who have reflected on the source of art have been distressed by a strange parasitism: all the arts seem to depend in large measure upon human suffering. The tragic pattern repeats itself: if we strive for great art, we must exploit and welcome the inhumanity of man to man. And it is more than a romantic legend to represent many artists as relying on their own suffering for the creative act. The unhappy Tennyson was a great poet; satisfied and at peace, he became, in Fitzgerald's phrase, a poetic machine. But not only artists: men in any profession may have to pay for success with a terrible hurt to another part of themselves. Tragic situations are so much taken for granted in our thinking—who does not know that men blindly persevere in professions for which they have no talent, or that they love on where they cannot be loved in return?—that to speak of them aloud is to belabor the commonplace. But then, as we have seen, to make the commonplace come alive—"to give," in Coleridge's words, "the charm of novelty to things of every day"—is one of the abiding goals of art.

We can go further. Aldous Huxley, in *Brave New World*, discovered that happiness itself is a blight, and that all the emotions that we really cherish derive from our misery. Not only the aesthetic experience, but love and pity and courage and admiration imply the existence of evil. We reach therefore the paradoxical condition of welcoming pain; and the hero of the novel turns into a flagellant! Anatole France arrives at the same conclusion regarding pain: "We owe to it all that is good in us, all that gives value to life," he writes in *Le Jardin d'Epicure*. There is then scarcely a virtue in our lives which does not require us to demand, if not to love, the presence of evil. This condition can actually be stated in two manners. If we begin with the desire for good—say a wish to write immortal poetry, or to love like Antony—then we face the tragic requisite of evil somehow and somewhere, for a blithe person in a blithe world will not write immortal poetry or love like Antony. Fortunately we can reverse the statement, and beginning with an evil we can say that it may often involve an inevitable good fortune. *"La fin du bien est un mal,"* goes one of La Rochefoucauld's posthumous maxims, *"et la fin du mal est un bien"*—"the end of a good is an evil, and the end of an evil is a good." [2] Perhaps this is not necessarily a cheering thought, but it cannot be denied that a villain may attempt a villainous deed, and by the nature of the drive and the context emerge unavoidably with a good. Political life is particularly susceptible to this species of tragedy-in-reverse: witness the good which, all historians agree, came of the Crusades.

In Anatole France's little book there is an entertaining story concerning the shade of Cadmus, come to visit the author in his library. The Phoenician is a rough and unprincipled captain, whose sole occupation while he lived was self-enrichment. He did not scruple to loot old treasures and massacre the innocents; but in his avidity for more wealth, he also found it useful to improve on the cumbersome method of writing (hence of keeping accounts) which was then current. In a word, in order to satisfy his rapacity, he invented the alphabet. The moral is that somewhere in the chain of events that leads to any object there is good and there is evil, take the words in almost any sense. And whether we have tragedy or tragedy-in-reverse often depends only on the point at which we break the chain.

2 In contrast with Cardinal Newman: "Good is not only good, but reproductive of good; this is one of its attributes; nothing is excellent, beautiful, perfect, desirable for its own sake, but it overflows, and spreads the likeness of itself around it." (*The Idea of a University*, VII, 5.)

This leads us to the final point that tragedy does not exhaust life, even though it is a condition of life. Life itself is stalked by death, but life is made up of many lives, as it were: it is constituted by a series of experiences. Sartre has made an attempt to prove that every act in this series is an expression of its own futility. Common experience refutes him. Futility is a judgment, and we know that many people do not judge their action as futile, whatever the philosopher may say. Sartre then accuses these people of being *salauds*, which is usually translated as "stinkers," but is rendered better by the vulgar "bastards." With this, however, the argument comes to an end, and each side withdraws to its fortifications, the bastards simply refusing to experience the suffering which the philosopher assures them they ought to feel.

Tragedy involves suffering. What men feel to be successful actions cannot be argued away as such on ontological grounds; success, indeed, is the feeling of success. The real tragedies we have touched on in this section involve felt, not theoretical, failure. Death itself is not necessarily an evil. Only those who hate and fear it can say that it is the fundamental blight of life; only for them is life tragic at the root. The great paradox is that the less tragic a man's life has been, the more tragic is the fact of death. Death is bitter only because life was good. But if that is so, the tragic view of life can be, as we maintained before, only one of the aspects under which life is considered. Were every act doomed to tragic failure, life as such would no longer be tragic, for we should be forced into the odd position that its inevitable consequence, death, was the basic victory of man.

Arestad, S., "Ibsen's Concept of Tragedy," *PMLA*, LXXIV (1959), 285–97.
Aristotle, the *Poetics*.
Bell, C. G., "Tragedy," *Diogenes*, No. 7 (1954), 12–32.
Bodkin, M., *Archetypal Patterns in Poetry*, Oxford, 1934.
Boileau, *L'Art poétique*.
Bradley, A. C., "Hegel's Theory of Tragedy," in *Oxford Lectures on Poetry*, second edition, London, 1920.
Bradley, A. C., *Shakespearean Tragedy*, New York, 1949.
Brunetière, F., *L'Evolution d'un genre: la tragédie*, in *Etudes critiques sur l'histoire de la littérature française*, seventh series, second edition, Paris, 1905.
Butcher, S. H., *Aristotle's Theory of Poetry and Fine Arts*, fourth edition, New York, 1951.
Campbell, L., *Tragic Drama in Aeschylus, Sophocles, and Shakespeare*, New York, 1904.
Clay, J. H., "A New Theory of Tragedy: a Description and Evaluation," *Educational Theatre Journal*, VIII (1956), 295–305.
Corneille, P., *Discours de la tragédie* and *Discours de l'utilité et des parties du poëme dramatique*, in *Oeuvres*, Volume 1, Paris, 1862.
Courtney, W. L., *The Idea of Tragedy in Ancient and Modern Drama*, New York, 1900.
Crocker, L. G., "Mr. Bell on Tragedy," *Diogenes*, No. 15 (1956), 112–20.
Dixon, W. M., *Tragedy*, third edition, London, 1929.
Ekeberg, G. W., *The English Novel as a Vehicle for Tragedy: Richardson through Hardy*, unpublished thesis, University of Wisconsin, 1942.
Else, G. F., *Aristotle's Poetics: the Argument*, Harvard, 1957.
Falk, E. H., *Renunciation as a Tragic Focus*, University of Minnesota, 1954.
Farnham, W., *The Medieval Heritage of Elizabethan Tragedy*, Berkeley, California, 1936.

Fontenelle, *Réflexions sur la poétique,* in *Oeuvres,* Volume 3, Paris, 1818.
Frye, N., *Anatomy of Criticism,* Princeton, 1957.
Greene, W. C., *Moira: Fate, Good, and Evil in Greek Thought,* Cambridge, Mass., 1944.
Hegel, G. W. F., *The Philosophy of Fine Arts,* translated by F. P. B. Osmaston, Volume 4, London, 1920.
Henn, T. R., *The Harvest of Tragedy,* London, 1956.
Herder, J. F., *Adrastea,* Volume 2, Part IV, in *Sämmtliche Werke,* Volume 23, Berlin, 1885.
Hume, D., "Of Tragedy," in *Essays Moral, Political, and Literary,* edited by Green and Grose, Volume 1, London, 1907.
Jarrett, J. L., "Tragedy, a Study in Explication," *ETC,* XII (1955), 189–97.
Jaspers, K., *Tragedy Is Not Enough (Uber das Tragische),* Boston, 1952.
Jepsen, L., *Ethical Aspects of Tragedy,* Gainesville, Florida, 1953.
Krieger, M., "Tragedy and the Tragic Vision," *Kenyon Review,* XX (1958), 281–99.
Krutch, J. W., *The Modern Temper,* New York, 1929.
Langer, S. K., *Feeling and Form,* New York, 1953.
Lesser, S. O., "Tragedy, Comedy, and the Esthetic Experience," *Literature and Psychology,* VI (1956), 131–39.
Lessing, G. E., *Dramatic Notes (Hamburgische Dramaturgie)* in *Selected Prose Works,* translated by Beasley and Zimmern, London, 1900.
Lucas, F. L., *Tragedy in Relation to Aristotle's Poetics,* London, 1927.
Maeterlinck, M., "Le Tragique quotidien," in *Le Trésor des humbles,* Paris, 1901.
Mann, O., *Poetik der Tragödie,* Bern, 1958.
McCollom, W. G., *Tragedy,* New York, 1957.
Morrell, R., "The Psychology of Tragic Pleasure," *Essays in Criticism* (Oxford), VI (1956), 22–37.
Muller, H. J., *The Spirit of Tragedy,* New York, 1956.
Murray, A. V., "Divine Tragedy," *Hibbert Journal,* LIII (1954), 19–24.
Murray, G., *The Classical Tradition in Poetry,* Harvard University, 1930.
Myers, H. A., *Tragedy: A View of Life,* Ithaca, New York, 1956.
Nicoll, A., *The Theory of Drama,* London, 1931.
Nietzsche, F., *The Birth of Tragedy from the Spirit of Music,* translated by C. Fadiman, in *The Philosophy of Nietzsche,* New York (Modern Library), 1937.
O'Neill, Jr., E., General Introduction to *The Complete Greek Drama,* Volume 1, New York, 1938.

Philipson, M. H., "Some Reflections on Tragedy," *Journal of Philosophy*, LV (1958), 197–203.
Pottle, F. A., "Catharsis," *Yale Review*, XL (1951), 621–41.
Racine, *Oeuvres Complètes*, Volume 1, Paris (Pléiade), 1956.
Ransom, J. C., *The World's Body*, New York, 1938.
Richards, I. A., *Principles of Literary Criticism*, fifth edition, New York, 1934.
Roberts, P., "A Christian Theory of Dramatic Tragedy," *Journal of Religion*, XXXI (1951), 1–20.
Robertson, J. G., *Lessing's Dramatic Theory*, Cambridge, 1939.
Schelling, F. W. J. von, *Philosophie der Kunst*, in *Werke*, Volume 3, Leipzig, 1907.
Schiller, *Über den Grund des Vergnügens an tragischen Gegenständen, and Uber die tragische Kunst*, in *Sämtliche Werke*, Volume 13, Stuttgart and Berlin (Cotta'sche Bibliothek), n.d.
Schlegel, A. W., *Lectures on Dramatic Art and Literature*, translated by J. Black, London, 1883.
Schopenhauer, A., *The World as Will and Idea*, translated by Haldane and Kemp, third edition, London, 1896.
Schwartz, E., "Detachment and Tragic Effect," *College English*, XVIII (1956), 153–56.
Sewall, R., "Vision of Tragedy," *Review of Metaphysics*, X (1956), 193–200.
Sidney, *Defence of Poesie*, in *Complete Works of Sir Philip Sidney*, edited by A. Feuillerat, Volume 3, Cambridge University Press, 1923.
Smart, J. S., "Tragedy," *Essays and Studies*, VIII (1922), Oxford, 9–36.
Stolnitz, J., "Notes on Comedy and Tragedy," *Philosophy and Phenomenological Research*, XVI (1955), 45–60.
Thorndike, A. H., *Tragedy*, Boston and New York, 1908.
Vaughan, C. E., *Types of Tragic Drama*, London, 1908.
Volkelt, J., *Asthetik des Tragischen*, second edition, Munich, 1906.
Wasserman, E. R., "The Pleasures of Tragedy," *ELH*, XIV (1947), 283–307.
Weisinger, H., *Tragedy and the Paradox of the Fortunate Fall*, Michigan State College, 1953.
Yeats, W. B., "The Tragic Theatre," in *The Cutting of an Agate*, New York, 1912.

Index